Nature Walks of Central Park

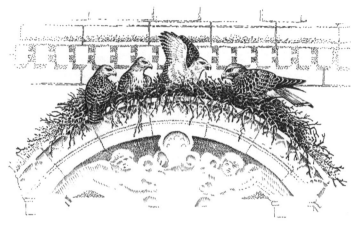

Red-tailed hawk family

NATURE WALKS OF

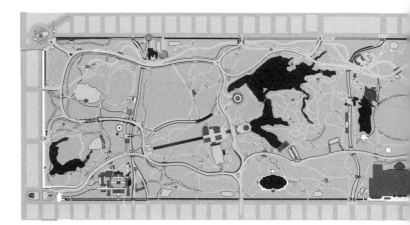

A John Macrae Book

Henry Holt and Company • New York

DENNIS BURTON

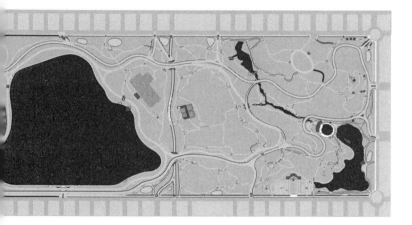

CENTRAL PARK

Botanical drawings by Charles Sprague Sargent
Bird drawings by Alan Messer

Henry Holt and Company, Inc.
Publishers since 1866
115 West 18th Street
New York, New York 10011

Henry Holt® is a registered trademark of Henry Holt and Company, Inc.

Published in Canada by Fitzhenry & Whiteside Ltd.,
195 Allstate Parkway, Markham, Ontario L3R 4T8.

Library of Congress Cataloging-in-Publication Data
Burton, Dennis
     Nature walks of Central Park / Dennis Burton.—First Owl book
ed.
        p.   cm.
     "A John Macrae book."
     Includes index.
     1. Natural history—New York (State)—New York—Guidebooks.
2. Nature trails—New York (State)—New York—Guidebooks.
3. Walking—New York (State)—New York—Guidebooks.   4. Central
Park (New York, N.Y.)—Guidebooks.   I. Title.
QH105.N7B87   1997   96-45269
508.747'1—dc21   CIP

ISBN 0-8050-4617-8

Henry Holt books are available for special
promotions and premiums. For details contact:
Director, Special Markets.

First Owl Book Edition—1997

Designed by Paula R. Szafranski

Printed in the United States of America
All first editions are printed on acid-free paper. ∞

10   9   8   7   6   5   4   3   2   1

To Mary

who makes all things

possible for me

Contents

Acknowledgments

THIS BOOK WOULD not have been possible without the help and support of the Central Park Conservancy and the New York City Parks Department's staff who offered both information and encouragement as I prepared these tours.

I especially wish to thank Karen Putnam, who is guiding Central Park into the next millennium; Marianne Cramer, whose dedication to and love and knowledge of Central Park I can compare to that of Olmsted, Vaux, and Parsons; Neil Calvanese, who reigns over the plant kingdom in Central Park; Sarah Cedar Miller, the park's photographer and knowledgeable historian; and Richard Kruzansky, whose unique understanding of Central Park's water bodies helped to shape these tours.

And I offer thanks to my friends who tested the tours and helped to edit the text, especially Regina Ryan, Sally Lee, Lynne Epple, David Chadwick, Rob Niosi, Dirk Keysser, Brenda Oppermann, Ronda Wingfield, Margie Salvante, Randy McCann, Alison Salzinger, and Hiroko Kiiffner. A very special thanks to Theo Coates for graphic and computer support; and to Jack Macrae, who edited the final text and came up with the idea for this book in the first place.

The botanical drawings are taken from *Manual of the Trees of North America* by Charles Sprague Sargent, with the kind permission of John Sargent.

The bird drawings are by Alan Messer.

D.B.
November 15, 1996

A portion of the proceeds of this book helps support the Central Park Conservancy in its efforts to preserve and maintain Central Park.

Introduction

> It is one great purpose of the Park to supply to the
> hundreds and thousands of tired workers, who have
> no opportunity to spend their summers in the coun-
> try, a specimen of God's handiwork that shall be to
> them, inexpensively, what a month or two in the
> White Mountains or the Adirondacks is, at great
> cost, to those in easier circumstances.
>
> FREDERICK LAW OLMSTED

WRITING THIS BOOK in 1996, I was fortunate to witness the
final phase of the fifteen-year-long restoration of Central Park.
Through its 139-year history, the park has undergone only one
other complete overhaul, during Robert Moses's tenure as Park
Commissioner in the 1930s. In addition, numerous piecemeal
restorations have stitched together the park's landscapes as
they became worn and torn by 20 million visitors each year.

Although some see Central Park as a permanent living
work of art, the only thing permanent about any landscape is
change. Beyond the seasonal and life-cycle changes common
to all living things, Central Park must also adapt to changing
tastes in park design, as well as political and economic reali-
ties. Frederick Law Olmsted and Calvert Vaux designed the
park after the English pastoral and picturesque landscapes
that were popular in the nineteenth century, with one dynamic
thought to formality, in the Mall. Yet, as styles changed, so did
the landscape designs of the park. Before leaving office, poli-
ticians of every administration imposed their own styles,

installing statuary and buildings, which, according to some sensibilities, cluttered the landscape. Now those buildings and statuary are integral to the park.

The latest restoration of Central Park, begun in 1980 and sponsored and maintained in large part by the Central Park Conservancy, reaches beyond simple renovation and general aesthetics into a dynamic relationship with the environment. Landscape designs of the past were often intended for instant gratification, to please the aesthetic eye, and after a few years of wear and tear, parks would have to be redesigned. This is not to say that landscape aesthetics are not noble and just in themselves or that function should override beauty, but a new sensibility, an urgency about the state of our environment, has developed in recent decades and has found its way into the design philosophy of many urban parks. Habitats are better understood today, and there is a growing tendency to favor native over exotic plantings (especially flora that attracts and sustains resident and migratory birds).

The intent of the walking tours in this book is to familiarize the visitor with not only the flora and fauna of Central Park but also with a history of its landscape design and cultural significance. In so doing I make use of information as far afield from Central Park as William K. Stevens's *Miracle Under the Oaks,* an account of the restoration of tall grass prairie remnants in the Chicago suburbs; Edward O. Wilson's urgent cry from the wilderness in the troubled rain forests; and Aldo Leopold's appeal in his *Round River* essays for a conservation ethic. Yet because this book is about Central Park, these reflections on the environment are intended to remind us that we are part of the natural world.

Central Park, if only nominally, is a remnant of Manhattan Island's natural history, a retreat from Gotham to the country, and, equally, a symbol of the environment: trod upon, abused, limited, and in constant need of care. This book represents

Central Park's beauty and its blemishes, but emphasizes its vitality and its necessity to New York. As battle lines are defined in the environmental argument, Central Park, sometimes boisterously, sometimes sedately, goes on about its business of supplying nature to the least natural environment on the planet: New York City.

Before you begin the walks, consider the following guidelines to make the Central Park experience easier, safer, and certainly more enjoyable.

Landmarks

Unlike other great works of art, Central Park is constantly changing. As the tastes of one generation fade into the next, so do such transitory park landmarks as sculpture, playgrounds, buildings, entrances, and even entire landscapes. For more than three generations, even though their style has changed, the park's lampposts have remained relatively permanent and numbered. Therefore, whenever available, the tours will incorporate them to guide the visitor. Most lampposts are embossed with locator numbers.

The first two numbers indicate the nearest street, so that lampposts #9200, #9202, or #9204 are between 92nd and 93rd Streets. Lamppost numbers such as 0300, 0302, or 0304 are between 103rd and 104th Streets. The last number indicates you are still close by the street named, and usually—but not always—north of the street "named" by the first two or three digits.

Because some lampposts were added after the initial numbering system, lighting engineers assigned new numbers according to their own system, such as #6-33 on the 100th Street Pool Walk and #N224 on the 59th Street Pond Walk. It is not necessary to understand those systems to orient yourself along the walks.

Blooms

Different species of trees, shrubs, wildflowers, and grasses will flower consistently within a week or so from year to year. Cooler winters will delay the blooms, but rarely for more than a week. Warmer springs may enhance blooms, but also not by more than a week. So the first week of April promises a continuous profusion of daffodils; the second week a long blast of magnolias; by the end of April the momentous flowering of the crab apples; and on through the year with something always in flower, until November, when the asters have finished their bloom following the first frost. If you wish to time your walk to a particular flowering time, a bloom schedule of some common park plants is included in Appendix D.

Taxonomy

This book is not a botanical guide. Most plants can be identified by general characteristics: leaf shape, flower, bark, and structure. Line drawings of some common species are included as an aid to identification. Plant names are given with common name first, then the botanical name by genus and species: red oak, *Quercus rubra*. Some genera have characteristics so similar as to be indistinguishable to even the trained eye. These are identified by genus followed by the nonspecific sp. For instance, the three similar species of yew shrub in the park are noted as: yew, *Taxus* sp. In keeping with the spirit of the book's advocacy of restoration ecology, all illustrations are of native plants.

Safety

Central Park has a lingering reputation for danger from a time when the Parks Department was so strapped for funds that maintenance and security in the park were almost nonexistent. However, since 1980, when the Central Park Conservancy began its unique partnership with the Parks Department in the maintenance and restoration of Central Park, that has changed. A highly successful maintenance and security system now prevails throughout the park. Zone gardeners, amiable and helpful, work within most of the forty-nine zones of the park. The landscapes of the nine walks in this book are all tended by zone gardeners. The presence of the New York Police Department in Central Park has also greatly increased in recent years. Nonetheless, Central Park is located in an urban environment, and the visitor should exercise the same prudence as elsewhere in the city.

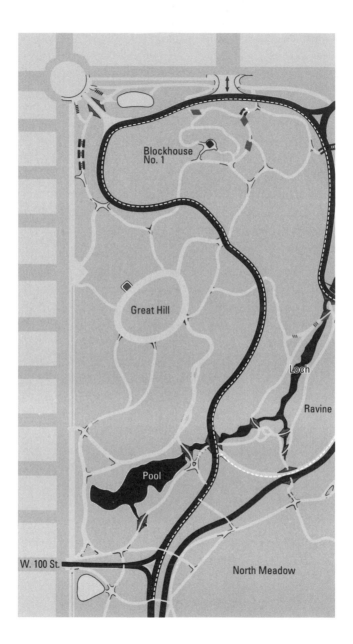

Pool Walk

100th Street Pool,
100th Street at Central Park West

BEGIN THIS WALK at the 100th Street entrance to Central Park on Central Park West. Stand on the north path by the wall and face into the park. Your first observation will be a sweep of turf and trees surrounding the 1.5-acre body of water known as The Pool. Set into the landscape around the Pool are many native and non-native trees, shrubs, and wildflowers. Central Park is home to 26,000 trees composed of 140 species, of which over twenty of the more prevalent species thrive around the Pool. This tour focuses on those trees and shrubs found commonly throughout the park and includes some specimens that were planted during the original landscaping in the mid-1800s.

For one hundred years the Pool contained over two acres of water, including a small island, but for reasons that remain obscure, half an acre of the Pool was filled in at the southwest corner and the island vanished after a severe winter storm in 1961.

The first tree on the left, between the stairs and the wall, is a medium-size Osage orange, *Maclura pomifera*. Sixty of these trees were registered in the *1982 Central Park Tree Inventory,* which counted 26,000 trees in Central Park over six inches in diameter. This medium-size Osage orange stands sentinel at the gate, welcoming visitors with its distinctive orange-hued bark. From October through December, the Osage orange has a grapefruit-size, crinkled yellow fruit that resembles the human brain. Many of the fruits that fall to the ground find their way into local kitchens as a purported control for cockroaches, although enough remain on the tree to be recognized as shriveled, brownish orange remnants through most of the winter.

The Osage orange is native to Oklahoma, home of the Osage Indians. The genus name, *Maclura,* honors William Maclure, a nineteenth-century American geologist, and the species name, *pomifera,* translates as pome-bearing, from the French *pome* for "apple," which includes most fleshy fruits with cores, such as pears, pomegranates, and Osage oranges. The Osage orange was introduced to Central Park by Frederick Law Olmsted and Calvert Vaux and, although scarcer in the park today than in 1982 (fewer than thirty now exist), a few large-diameter, stately specimens throughout the park are believed to be original park plantings.

Continue along the path to the right, not down the stairs. In early spring, a large swath of yellow daffodils and blue crocuses will be in bloom in the grassy slope to your left

Osage orange

along the staircase. Approximately at the line of 100th Street behind the first lamppost, #0001, and to the left, a crab apple, *Malus* sp., displays white flowers from late April through early May. The "flowering of the crabs," a welcome harbinger of fair weather, is a park-wide event keenly awaited by tens of thousands of New Yorkers. In 1982, more than four hundred crab apples graced the drives and pathways throughout the park, including two stunning allees in the Conservatory Garden, which we will visit on the Harlem Meer Walk. Along the East Drive, from 79th to 86th Streets, every bend in the road offers spectacular displays of shimmering rich pink and white crab apple blossoms. In their natural habitat, crab apples grow in wooded thickets and bottomlands where the soil is rich and moist. In autumn, the tiny apples are gathered for preserves and vinegar, and when tastier wild food is scarce, numerous songbirds eat the fruit, which often persists through the winter.

Beyond the crab apple, a series of three large black locust trees, *Robinia pseudoacacia,* loom up from the lawn, recognized by their deeply furrowed tan bark and twisted forms. In the *1982 Tree Inventory,* the black locusts were ranked fourth of all trees species in the park with over 1,600 specimens. The durable, tight-grained wood of the black locust makes excellent fences, which we shall see later on the Loch Walk. The renowned taxonomist Linnaeus bestowed the black locust with its genus name *Robinia* after Jean Robin, a seventeenth-century French herbalist, and his son, Vespasian, who cultivated the tree in Europe. Its common name, locust, comes by a wayward route: Because missionaries did not want to accept the fact that John the Baptist ate locusts (the grasshopper), they interpreted his food preference to be the fruit of the carob tree, also called locust, whose fleshy black pods, similar to the legume of our black locusts, vaguely resemble the insect. As a member of the *Lequminosae* family, it provides nitrogen to the soil and is frequently used to reclaim soil, especially on strip-mined sites. The tree's fragrant flowers are the basis of an excellent honey, and in the wild many animals, including bobwhite, pheasant, mourning dove, rabbits, and deer, browse the seeds. A magnificent and wonderfully fragrant stand of more than a dozen black locusts is encountered on the walk around the Harlem Meer.

Four black locusts grew on this slope until the early 1990s, but one of them was removed when its crown began dying back, often a sign of root damage, and the trees were considered hazardous. Root damage, usually caused by heavy foot traffic, construction, or droughty soils, restricts the flow of water and nutrients to the trees. All park users need to heed the warning: Don't step on anything green and stay on the paved paths.

At the first intersection next to the second lamppost, #6-33, a mature Norway maple, *Acer platanoides,* provides deep shade with its dense foliage. In 1982, Norway maples ranked sixth in the tree inventory with more than 1,300 specimens. Since then that number has been purposely reduced. Horticulturists in most urban parks, including Central Park, no longer plant Norway maples because they are "invasive aliens," spreading their vigorous seeds and seedlings and displacing native species. They proliferate in our ecosystems because they tolerate dry, shady soils and have few diseases or pests to check their growth. But the word has not spread much beyond the park system, and many nurseries sell more Norway maples than any other species of tree. Unless park policy changes, however, the Norway maple will be extinct in Central Park in approximately 150 years. But if it's a hot day and you're standing in the maple's cool shade, you will understand another reason for the maples' popularity.

Across the path on the right, on the small hill near the edge of the road, a stately horse chestnut tree, *Aesculus hippocastanum,* stands poised with four trunks growing from the main trunk. Besides the trunk it is also easily recognized by its five-bladed leaf configured somewhat like the spokes of a wheel. In 1982, 110 horse chestnuts were counted in Central Park with this particular tree cited in Louis Harmon Peet's 1903 book, *Trees and Shrubs of Central Park*. Peet's book, compiled thirty years after the completion of the park, assumes them to be original plantings. Though many of those trees have died, enough of them still exist to enrich us with a sense of the park's history.

This horse chestnut is not the spreading chestnut tree under which the village smithy stood in Longfellow's "The Village Blacksmith." That honor belongs to the American chestnut, *Castanea dentata*, which is virtually extinct because of a fungus, *Endothia parasitica*, introduced from Asia in 1910. The American chestnut once dominated our Eastern forest but now is limited to stump sprouts of ten to fifteen feet (the disease does not kill the roots). A small number of isolated trees escaped the blight and are spread sparsely throughout the northeast, some as close as Stokes National Forest in New Jersey. A vigorous campaign to cure the disease is under way by the American Chestnut Foundation.

The horse chestnut under which you are standing is not botanically a chestnut at all but a European member of our native buckeye family. A native sweet buckeye, *Aesculus glabra*, about the same age as the horse chestnut, can be seen directly across the road about thirty feet from the curb. The fruits of both buckeyes, which mature in September and October, reveal the immediate difference between the two species. The thorny husks covering the chestnut's nutlets resemble green land mines, while the sweet buckeye husks are smooth. In 1982, twenty-one sweet buckeyes were found in the park.

The next stop is just ahead near the water fountain, where the path branches to the right. A large smooth-leafed elm, *Ulmus carpinifolia*, grows beside the fountain. Its common name refers to its leaves, which are smoother to the touch than

Ohio buckeye

most other elm species. A comparison of the elm's bark and the horse chestnut's bark offers another means of identifying trees in winter, when fruit, flowers, or leaves are not available. The elm's bark has a uniform texture and is darker than the horse chestnut, whereas the horse chestnut bark is more scaly than the elm's.

In between the elm and the horse chestnut stands a European hornbeam, *Carpinus betulus,* a smaller tree, with smooth, steel-gray bark. The *1982 Tree Inventory* lists over two hundred hornbeams in the park. Another common name for this tree is ironwood—for its heavy, tough-as-nails wood; yet surprisingly the wood rots faster than most other species when it touches the ground. Among the wildlife that enjoy hornbeam seeds in late summer are the gray squirrel, ruffed grouse, bobwhite, pheasant, and wild turkey, of which only the gray squirrel is found abundantly in the park and why you may not see any seeds on this tree.

The walk now bears left along the path heading toward the water to lamppost #0015 through a stand of no less than thirteen London plane trees, *Platanus acerifolia,* ranked fifth in the tree survey of 1982 with over 1,300 specimens. Off to the left from the lamppost, in among the London plane trees, stands a lone American sycamore, *Platanus occidentalis,* between two boulders as you face the water of the pool. The sycamores totaled 106 specimens in 1982. Both the London plane and American sycamore have mottled bark; the American sycamore's lighter-colored bark with small, raised, dark blotches on the lower trunk distinguishes it from the London plane's smooth yellowish bark. The pendulous fruits, visible from October through much of the winter, offer the botanical difference between the two species. The American sycamore has a single, pendulous fruit ball while the London plane has two to four fruit balls hanging from a single stalk.

American sycamore

The London plane is a hybrid of the American sycamore and the Chinese sycamore, the latter not found in Central Park. Robert Moses, Parks Commissioner from 1930 until 1960, favored the London plane and planted them extensively, an act that would have outraged the park's original designers, who favored plant diversity and harmony with the landscape. Samuel Parsons, Central Park's superintendent from 1882 to 1911, put it so:

> Every tree or shrub employed in the Park should find
> place there only as it shows value in the whole unified

artistic effect. The fact that any plant has botanical interest should weigh not at all in its artistic employment. It is the hue and shape in the picture, the line in the horizon that we should always seek.

The tallest tree in the eastern United States is the American sycamore—175 feet with a diameter of fourteen feet. It is also the longest lived, at up to six hundred years. The one that rises majestically here, with the pool beyond, is a fine specimen, though not mature at less than one hundred years old and well under 100 feet high. The sycamore served colonists and Native Americans well: the sycamore's hardwood with its coarse grain was used for cabinets, barrels, furniture, and butcher blocks. Native Americans used its massive trunks for dugouts—one 65 feet long was reported to have weighed four and a half tons. In the wild, sycamores tower above rivers and lakes, providing nests and shelter to opossum, raccoons, and wood ducks, especially in hollowed branches of mature trees.

The path continues toward the sound of rushing water and a small cavern where the water cascades out and tumbles over glistening rocks. This is the main water source for the Pool fed by overflow from the Jacqueline Kennedy Onassis reservoir that keeps the Pool at a more or less constant level. After heavy rains the volume of the cascade increases, causing the tumbling water to spray mist up on the path—a cooling treat for passersby on a sweltering day after a late summer thunderstorm. The odor of chlorine often emanates from the cascade. Chlorine has been added to New York City's drinking water since 1910 (fluoridation of the water began in 1965) and the reservoir, fed from the Croton Aqueduct System, still receives chlorine even though it no longer serves water to the city.

The tour continues along to the end of the railing. Off to the right on the turf are a number of specimen trees. The tall,

Tulip tree

straight tree growing atop the cascade is one of four tulip trees, *Liriodendron tulipfera,* planted more or less in a circle. Tulip trees, also commonly known as tulip poplar or yellow poplar, are recognized even at a distance by their tall, straight trunks and dark gray-colored bark. Not related to true poplars, they are the second-largest tree in the East, growing occasionally, though not as frequently as the sycamore, to 165 feet and nearly 10 feet in diameter. The 1982 survey lists only 90 tulip trees, but they have been increasing in number. Unlike the pollution intolerant sycamore the shorter-lived tulip tree is one of the few desirable trees in the harsh, trampled soils of Central Park that regenerates naturally by growing from seed to towering tree. The first branch on mature tulip trees may not emerge until well over thirty feet above the ground. Unfortunately, the flowers, which bloom in late May and are among the loveliest of all native trees, are unobservable at that height. Linnaeus's fanciful Latin name for the tree translates as "tulip-bearing lily tree." As a member of the magnolia family, the flower is large, colorful, and fragrant, as you will see if you're lucky enough to find one on the ground after a squirrel or gust of wind has broken it off.

A specimen red maple, *Acer rubrum,* looms up on the lawn about thirty feet from the end of the pipe rail fence. You can recognize this maple by the striated gray bark, the somewhat exposed shallow roots above ground at its base, and the fan-lobed leaves. The maple's small, colorful flowers, not as individually showy as the tulip tree's, nonetheless cover its entire crown in March, offering some of the most distinctive bursts of color in late winter–early spring. This native maple poses no threat to the native ecology of our area. Unlike the Norway maple, it only occasionally regenerates in most urban parks. In order to reestablish the native plant palette in Central Park, the red maple, and many other nonregenerating native plants, must be purchased from nurseries. The park's current horticultural managers hope that by restoring at least a few landscapes of the park to native plants, as has been done in much of the north end of the park, the remnant native ecosystem will be at least partially resuscitated for future generations.

At the first set of benches, walk toward the peninsula jutting into the water past two black locusts. Another red maple stands off to the right. A weeping willow, *Salix babylonica,* grows near the water to the left of the red maple. In 1982, fifty-three weeping willows grew in the park. These willows are certainly the most recognizable willow species of the nearly seventy *Salix* species in the Northeast, four of which are found in the park. Weeping willows are commonly planted as accents around ponds and lakes. Their fluid, droopy habit and graceful reflection appear to grow both into and out of the water, making these fast-growing trees an all-round favorite in the landscape.

As you walk out on the peninsula, three young bald cypresses, *Taxodium distichum,* can be recognized by their short, deciduous needles, which are green on both sides, and by the light brown, smooth, fibrous bark with orange striations looking almost as if it were shredding. Their numbers have increased two-fold since 1982, when only fifteen were recorded in the tree survey. Another dozen or so have been planted since then in various restoration projects. The bald cypress's native habitat begins south of New Jersey, but they have been successfully introduced farther north and now grow into the more northern latitudes of New England. The park's threesome, planted in the 1980s, in time will have a striking command of the Pool with the trees' orange-rust autumn foliage accenting the water and the distant skyline. On the west edge of the Pool, a much larger bald cypress rises up to the left of another weeping willow, which we'll visit further along on the tour.

The peninsula promises to be a good bird-watching station year-round. Off to the left, the reeds growing out of the water are cattails, *Typha latifolia,* a favorite haunt of several species of waterfowl. The most common bird found on this water is the mallard duck, *Anas platyrhynchos,* a permanent resident of the park as well as the ancestor of our domestic ducks. In the winter, black ducks, *Anas rubipres,* join the mallards. In the wild the two species, each with a life span of about twenty-three years, occasionally mate to create black mallard hybrids, although there are no records of their mating in Central Park.

The autumn migration period, from August until November when weather turns sharply colder north of New York City, provides diverse bird-watching on all the water bodies in the park, and, with a little persistence, you might spot bufflehead, merganser, wood duck, scaup, ruddy duck, gadwalls, and many more. In spring and summer, black-crowned night herons can be seen standing patiently in the water waiting for a meal of small fish or crawdads. Both the great and snowy egrets occasionally stop off in the Pool or at the Harlem Meer to snatch a fish or two on their commute between the Hudson and the East Rivers. Egrets were nearly extinct at the turn of the century, due to feather poachers dealing in the millinery trade, but recovered after protective laws were passed in 1913.

Before returning to the path, note the sweet gum, *Liquidambar styraciflua,* leaning over the water to the right of the

Sweet gum

three cypress trees. This tree is recognized in summer by the flat-bottomed, star-shaped leaves and gray furrowed bark. One hundred and forty-two sweet gums occupied Central Park in 1982. In winter, the tree can be recognized by the prickly seed capsules that stay on it until December and, if not raked up, litter the ground beneath it until the summer, when their tough cellulose husks decay. Sweet gums are another of the many native trees offering both beauty and bounty. Their autumn foliage has various shades of yellows, oranges, and reds, often on the same tree. They grow quickly in moist woods but will grow on upland soil as well.

The common name sweet gum refers to the sap of the tree and its pleasant, unsugary taste; it was used as chewing gum by American colonists. The tree's lumber is still used for veneer, furniture, wooden bowls, boxes, toys, and boats. The seeds are a quality wildlife food. Many migratory songbirds as well as bobwhite, wild turkey, chipmunks, and gray squirrels readily gobble down the seeds.

Facing the next series of benches are a black locust with a girth of thirty inches, and a smaller locust to its right. Behind the locusts a stand of scraggly hawthorns, *Cratageus spp.*, do no justice to this otherwise attractive genus of small trees, in which Asa Gray's *Manual of Botany* lists 103 species with nearly as many varieties. The hawthorns are similar to the crab

apples in appearance and habit. Hawthorn flowers are, however, smaller and not as showy as the crab apples'. In 1982,
403 hawthorns of over six inches in diameter were counted in
the park, but there are certainly many more that are less than
six inches. (The crab apple-like fruits are discussed at length in
the Turtle Pond Walk.)

Immediately behind the bench, two ginkgo trees, *Ginkgo
bilboa,* bestow their antiquity on the diversity of the trees in
this area. The ginkgo's more flattering common name, maidenhair, refers to the southern maidenhair fern of the southern
United States, *Adiantum Capillus-Veneris,* whose leaves resemble the ginkgo's and whose branching pattern resembles the
artistically classic flow of a young maiden's hair. Yet there
should be no difficulty in recognizing the ginkgo by the leaves
alone, which, as far back as the eighth century, the Chinese
called "the tree with leaves like a duck's foot." The bark also
aids in identification, with its distinct light tones of brown and
gray etched with dark furrows.

The ginkgo's lineage can be traced back 30 million years to
the Mesozoic Era, which includes the Jurassic period of the
dinosaurs, when ferns, cyads, and palms dominated the forests.
Most of the ginkgo population was destroyed by glaciers over
15,000 years ago. The glaciers, covering as much as one-third
of the earth's surface, changed the structure of the planet's
forests by pushing them south. Today's forests emerged and
spread north after the last glacier receded. Some trees, such as
the ginkgo, did not fare as well in the postglacial period as
others did, such as the oaks and hickories. Only remnants of
the ginkgoes have survived since the last glacial period. Today
the ginkgo is the only surviving member of its *Ginkgaceae* family, which traces its ancestry to trees found in Buddhist monas-
teries in China and Japan in the 1800s. Ginkgoes no longer
grow in the wild but are widely planted as landscape and street
trees. During the Enlightenment of the eighteenth century, the

uniqueness of ginkgoes quickly caught on with European horticulturists, who believed that the diversity of shape and form in landscapes was as important as we believe native ecological diversity to be today.

Ginkgoes have a somewhat conical, scraggly habit before maturing into asymmetrically spreading trees up to eighty feet tall with crowns up to forty feet across. The wonderfully golden-yellow autumnal leaves drop and spread giltlike over the grass. (Two well-placed mature specimens can be viewed atop Cherry Hill at the end of the West Lake Walk.) The ginkgo's pollution tolerance is legendary and makes it a hardy street tree. Because they are ancient, ginkgoes have no pests or diseases surviving to interfere with them. The only significant problem with these trees in parks or on streets is the offensive odor of their fruit, which, when the wind is right, can be smelled from blocks away. Odor notwithstanding, some ethnic Chinese entrepreneurs gather the fruit, scrape off the pulp, and collect the nuts, which is said to be a delicacy after roasting.

On the right of the path, halfway to the next set of benches, a specimen native white oak, *Quercus alba,* with its distinctive flaky, light-colored bark, stands tall among its neighboring trees. Of the fourteen species of nearly five thousand oaks counted in the park in the 1982 survey, less than fifty were white oaks. Their landscape value, hardiness, and disease resistance warrant a wider distribution. This tree appears to be about ninety years old, and in a less stressful environment would probably live for three hundred years. In Central Park its life expectancy will be half that. Because white oak acorns contain less of the bitter tannins than most oaks, they are readily eaten by squirrels, birds, and other wildlife. In 1991 this tree dispersed hundreds of acorns. Within two weeks, only a few of those acorns could be found after the squirrels and blue jays cached them away. The tree produced no more acorns until 1996, which is typical of the white oak group, which has periods of heavy nut production every five or ten years. Indians boiled white oak acorns to remove the tannic acid and used the ground meal as a staple in their diet.

Twenty feet behind the white oak, look for a smaller pin oak, *Quercus palustris*. Its smooth gray bark displays flecks of orange as it ages. The 1982 survey ranked the pin oak as the third most common tree in the park, with over 1,700 specimens, constituting nearly 12 percent of all the park's trees. Once matured, the lower branches of pin oaks have a majestic sweep downward, somewhat resembling a ballerina's tutu. When these lower branches die, after about thirty years, they are usually pruned (an impressive specimen with its tutu intact will be encountered on the East Lake Walk). The common name pin refers to the wood, which makes sturdy carpenter's dowels used for fastening joints.

Continue on to the next intersection of paths, past the benches, where a sign indicates THE POOL on an unnumbered lamppost. One path goes to the right, another declines down a short set of three stairs, and the other leads us left across a rustic foot bridge. The path down the steps begins the Loch Walk through the North Woods Ravine, the second water body tour.

The Pool Walk continues across the foot bridge beyond two more weeping willows on the water's edge. Immediately across the bridge on the left, a picturesque black locust with two trunks twists out over the water. Given its size, this tree was probably planted in the 1960s. Black locusts self-seed readily, but when encountered in mowed, grassy areas, it is safe to assume that they were intentionally placed in the landscape.

The large American sycamore on the left displays the grandeur of the species' lofty trunk and ample diameter. Placed here, with no other trees to interfere with it, as the London planes do across the water, it excels in the landscape and greatly enhances the shore of the Pool.

On the water's edge of this promontory, across the path from lamppost #0218, a statuesque red maple leans severely over the water. Peet's 1903 book describes a red maple on this spot; however, red maples are short-lived, and that tree would certainly have succumbed to age by now. It's more likely that this tree replaces the original tree mentioned by Peet. During the various administrations supervising the plantings in Central Park, some were blessed with prescient horticulturists who adhered to Olmsted and Vaux's vision of properly placing trees and shrubs to attain specific effects. As part of that horticultural maintenance, they replaced the senescent plants with younger successors. This red maple's brilliant autumnal colors express the artistry of such landscape designing.

Farther along on the waterside and across the path from lamppost #0219, a pignut hickory, *Carya glabra,* divides its smooth gray trunk ten feet above the ground. Six species of hickory, totaling 185 trees, were listed in the 1982 survey. The regenerating bitternut hickory was the most common species, with 77 specimens, while the pignut was second with 40 specimens. Fewer pignuts survive today because they rarely regenerate in the park—their nuts are quickly eaten by squirrels that reject the bitternut hickory fruit.

Where the path divides at lamppost #0213, a green ash, *Fraxinus pennsylvanica,* leans out from the lawn. The fur-

Pignut hickory

rowed, crosshatched bark with patterns of chevrons and attenuated diamonds distinguishes it from the surrounding trees. The compound leaves with seven to nine leaflets also aid in identification. In October–November, ashes produce thousands of stiff, wedge-shaped fruits equipped with sharp points, often found impaled in leaves on lower shrubs or littering park paths. Of the two species of ash in Central Park, the white ash, *Fraxinus americana,* is the more common, with 837 specimens counted in 1982; the green ash numbered only 180. The green ash grows naturally in lowlands, in moister, fertile soil, much lacking in the park, although this specimen is well placed here near the Pool.

The ash figures prominently in Teutonic mythology. In the primeval forests of northern Europe the Norse people believed that the unnamed Supreme Deity, who created Odin, their principal god, also created Yggdrasil, the mighty ash tree, to support the sky. Yggdrasil's roots extended deep into the earth (as indeed the ash's do) and integrated time, life, and destiny. The trunk rose through the realm of man and branched upward into the heavens, so far into the heavens that they even cast a shadow on Odin's palace. Below the earth, the three Fates watered the roots and kept them safe from Nidhug, the dragon, who gnawed continually at the tree of life. But the care given by the Fates negated the harm done by the dragon. One day, while strolling on the beach, Odin picked up some driftwood—a branch of the ash—and created the first man.

Where the paths intersect after the row of benches, the first tree on the left is a small sugar maple, *Acer saccharum,* whose trunk splits about eight feet up from its base. Fifty sugar maples were recorded in the *1982 Tree Inventory.* Sugar maples receive mixed reviews from ecologists and foresters. They are, along with the red maple, the major contributor to the spectacular colors of the Northeast's autumnal foliage, but they also sprout like weeds in dense shade and displace other

Sugar maple

tree species, most notably the oaks and hickories. Ecologists classify the sugar maple as a "gap species," because it grows rapidly in the gaps where the tree canopy has been opened, allowing sunlight to reach the maple seedlings. The seedlings tolerate deep shade, growing very slowly until such openings vitalize them. Seedling growth has been known to be suppressed for up to a hundred years, after which they opportunistically fill the canopy when an opening occurs. A healthy sugar maple can live for up to two hundred years.

Sugar maples have always grown in the oak-hickory forest but have never approached dominance until this century. Now they are increasing rapidly and could possibly become dominant in the oak-hickory forest's northern range. The sugar maples' shade tolerance and strong resistance to catastrophic winds favor their growth over the oaks and hickories.

The oak-hickory forest, the largest forest type on the East Coast, was created over many centuries by the regular burning of the forests by Native Americans. In this century, the suppression of fire has resulted in the increased distribution of sugar maples. What this means to the future of eastern forests may not be known for several generations. In recent decades the disadvantages of fire suppression have become more clear as aggressive species, such as sugar maple, take advantage of the fireless environment. Many restoration ecologists now use fire as it was used by Native Americans and by nature, through lightning, to maintain ecosystems.

The final tree on this tour is the bald cypress, *Taxodium distichum,* near the shoreline across from the numberless lamppost on the right. Three younger bald cypresses were examined along the south shore of the Pool on this tour. Although this is not an original planting, Vaux and Olmsted did relish the bald cypress for its dramatic vertical accent and seasonal diversity. In the nineteenth century, hundreds of these trees decorated the park. Unfortunately, the abuses of trampling and horticultural neglect have killed most of them. This specimen is perfectly placed here along the edge of the Pool so that the tree's knobby root growths, known as "knees," are growing in and along the edge of the water. It is believed that the knees bring oxygen to the cypress, which often grows partially submerged in swamps.

Bald cypress swamps make up a forest type of their own, ranging along the coastal plain from Maryland to Florida and west to Texas. In these swamps many of America's spectacular animals find refuge. Among them are the coypu, a large southern version of the muskrat introduced from South America for its fur; marsh rabbit, a fine swimmer, found almost exclusively in the Dismal Swamp of Virginia; and bobcats and cougars, North America's striking wild cats. Many bird species also

Bald cypress

thrive in these swamps, including prothonotary warblers, herons, egrets, barred owls, wood ducks, ibis, yellow-billed cuckoos, pileated woodpeckers, and now, only rarely, in the remotest areas, the ivory-billed woodpecker. The ivory-billed woodpecker is the largest of America's woodpeckers and, arguably, the most attractive, although it is heading for extinction due to the destruction of its habitat. The cypress swamps may also be destined for that same fate. Central Park's urban forest, some of it a remnant of the Colonial forest, reflects the need for restoration and preservation of America's hallowed and diminishing wildland.

The Pool tour ends ahead, at the steps that lead back to Central Park West.

Loch Walk

The Loch,
West Drive at 102nd Street

THIS WALK BEGINS at the northwest corner of the West 100th Street entrance to the park. Follow the path along the north side of the Pool to the unnumbered lamppost with a sign reading THE POOL. Along the walk we will observe a wildflower meadow, a series of cascades, a gravity bridge, a rock bridge, a rustic bridge, and, known simply as the North Woods, the least urban environment in the entire park. No lampposts guide this tour; however, enough permanent landmarks, bridges, cascades, and stairs exist to keep you from getting lost.

Before going down the three steps leading to Glen Span Arch, pause a moment to survey the Pool and its formal landscape spreading out to Central Park West. The appearance of the landscape will change here from that of a managed parkscape, with intentionally placed trees and shrubs, to the rougher aspect of a rural woods.

Follow the path down to the first set of two small steps. On the left of the path look up at a venerable tulip tree, *Liriodendron tulipfera*. Most mature tulip trees are easily recognized

21

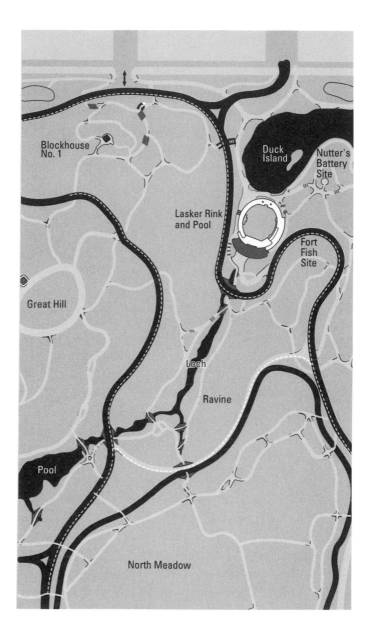

by their breadth, height, and straight trunks rocketing skyward. Louis Harmon Peet mentions this tulip in his 1903 book, *Trees and Shrubs of Central Park*, which means that it may have been planted in the 1860s or 1870s when the park was being constructed. However, because of the tulip's age and the stress it endures on this dry slope surrounded by asphalt, this tree may not survive many more droughty summers or stormy winters.

Continue down over two more small steps and pause on the rock platform at the water's edge to take in the sound of the cascade, which is amplified in this small gorge. The overall effect removes the park user from the sights and sounds of the city. Before construction of the park began, this water course was known as Montayne's Rivulet, after the Montayne family who owned farmland in the vicinity. At that time the rivulet began where today Columbus Avenue and 95th Street connect and flowed north and west to empty into Harlem Creek (the present day Harlem Meer). The 100th Street Pool and the cascade were created by damming Montayne's Rivulet with boulders and soil. This cascade will be the first of three encountered on the tour.

In 1990, the Central Park Conservancy undertook the restoration of the cascade, the steep slope across the water, and Glen Span Arch on the right. Many years of erosion and decaying stone had changed the appearance of this picturesque location. Using photographs from the 1800s, the Conservancy's landscape designers recreated the original configuration of the cascade and stream banks by repositioning the boulders, many of which had tumbled into the water.

Across the water, along the craggy slope, evergreen ferns set into the rocks offer a splash of winter verdure and soften the coarse texture of the rocks and wintry shrubs. In spring and summer, scan among the rocks on the slope for sweet pepperbush, *Clethra alnifolia*, a colonizer of stream banks and damp thickets. This spindly shrub is one of the few species in our area to blossom in late July, offering a profusion of tiny flowers on attractive white spikes that emanate a most pleasant fragrance, giving the shrub its second common name, summersweet. The seed pods, resembling peppercorns, remain on the shrub through the winter.

Higher up on the slope across the water, the large tree spreading over the crest is a white ash, *Fraxinus americana,* growing, as it does in the wild, upland, high and dry. In the shade of the white ash look for winterberry, *Ilex verticillata,*

White ash

another attractive shrub related to the familiar Christmas holly. The winterberry and the two white pines, *Pinus strobus,* on top of the ridge, are recent additions to the original Winter Drive, a stretch of the park that ran from 100th Street down to approximately 77th Street, featuring evergreen trees and shrubs with appealing fruit and foliage in the winter months. Many of the Winter Drive plantings had succumbed to neglect and pollution, so in the early 1990s the Central Park Conservancy began replanting the drive with hardier, more urban-tolerant tree and shrub species. Pines eventually languish near the perimeter walls of the park, where constant automobile exhaust injures them, but here, closer to the center of the park, these pines should persevere for many years.

Move ahead to the bridge. From this point a striking view of the woodlands is framed as you look through Glen Span Arch. This effect of framing the changing landscape was intentional. Olmsted and Vaux designed many of the bridges and arches in the park as portals from one landscape experience to another. From here, the bridge moves us out of the manicured parkscape of the Pool to the rural experience of the woodlands. This arch, named Glen Span because it traverses this glen, was originally a wood-slat bridge designed and built in 1863 by Calvert Vaux and Jacob Wrey Mould, who designed many of the other bridges and structures in Central Park. In 1885, the wooden slats were removed and changed to a sturdier design of macadam and stone to accommodate more traffic. The original wood-slat design allowed sunlight to dapple into the grotto beneath the bridge where mosses and ferns were planted on the boulders and ledges. An irrigation system from above supplied water to the plants, which could be enjoyed by visitors sitting on the wooden bench that once occupied the niche on the south edge of the path. The irrigation system remains, but the grotto now lacks the sunlight to grow plants.

Continue under the arch, with the sound of the cascade diminishing behind you. Notice the pleasant shift of resonance from the soothing cascade to the invigorating music of birdsong and wind in the woodland trees. During construction of the Park, little change occurred to the Loch landscape. The word *loch* comes from the Scottish word for lake, which this water body more closely resembled in the nineteenth century before eighty years of siltation pinched it into this narrow stream. Olmsted and Vaux intended this woodland, through which the Loch flows before it empties into the Harlem Meer, to have the rustic and rugged appearance it has today. Photographs taken at the end of the nineteenth century show the trees in the Ravine to be much smaller than they are now.

Ironically, the trees around the Loch are larger today than they have been since the Revolutionary War.

Across the water, along the bank, an erosion control project has been successful and easy to maintain because trampling is minimal on the steep little slope. In the center of the bank, a dense planting of the vine Virginia creeper, also known as woodbine, *Parthenocissus quinquefolia,* recognized by the five-bladed leaf that resembles the horse chestnut leaf, stabilizes the soil. The vine is commonly found in woods along rocky stream banks, and for that reason was chosen for this site. Scattered over the rest of the slope, cranberry viburnum, bottlebrush grass, blue and white asters, ferns, snakeroot, and more are on display throughout the year.

Just off the path on the left, before the paths diverge, examine the exposed roots and lower trunk of a large black willow, *Salix nigra,* that blew down in a storm in 1993. The trunk and branches were removed from the path, but the stump was left to contribute to the woodland aesthetic and offer habitat and forage for wildlife. A number of black willows were planted along this stream in the 1940s. As they succumb to age and storms and fall to the ground, they open the tree canopy and allow sunlight to reach the lower vegetation along the stream banks. The park's woodland management team takes advantage of this by planting thickets of streamside plants that both attract wildlife and diversify the park's 90 acres of woodlands.

Along the rest of the tour an abundance of woodland wildflowers may be found. Because of the unpredictable nature of pedestrian traffic trampling the flowers, it is suggested that no one venture off the paths to find them: off-path traffic is responsible for their demise. That said, stay alert to the many grasses, forbs, and ferns that do survive here. A partial list of a few hardy species includes: Allegheny spurge, *Pachysandra procumbens,* our native pachysandra, with attractive spikes of salmon-colored flowers that appear in early April; Virginia bluebells, *Mertensia virginica,* a springtime ephemeral plant flowering in late April and gone, flowers, leaves, and all, by mid-May; violets, *Viola spp.,* blue, white, and bicolored varieties; woodland phlox, *Phlox divaricata,* with delicate blue flowers in early May; wild geraniums, *Geranium maculatum,* wildly pink in mid-May; alumroot, *Heuchera americana,* with its slender spikes of tiny, drooping flowers and red-tinged petals in late May and well beyond; blue flag iris, *Iris versicolor,* growing near and often in the water with long, sword-shaped leaves and showy violet-blue flowers in early June; and many others, existing at this writing, which may or may not survive the long run of intense urban park use.

In the oval circle where the paths converge, examine the two red oaks, *Quercus rubra,* with majestic trunks. Louis Harmon Peet mentioned these trees in his 1903 book. It's possible that they existed before the park was constructed and the path was built around them. These excellent specimens display the red oak's mature form and patterns, though they are beginning to decline. Notice the stripes, sometimes called "ski trails," running from about thirty feet aboveground to the top of the tree. This is a classic red oak bark pattern and distinguishes it from its close relative, the black oak, *Quercus velutina,* which has darker bark broken into small patches. The trunk of a small black oak that died in 1995 occupies the next circle along the path. The dead trunk, called a snag, is left standing for wildlife to forage and nest; it also allows us to compare the bark of these two oaks. This black oak snag should stand for many more years, but if it doesn't, other black oaks, larger and healthier, will be seen farther along.

To the left another rustic bridge crosses the water. We'll visit that bridge at the end of the tour. But straight ahead yet another rustic bridge crosses a small stream, which is often dry in late summer. About twenty feet before the bridge, a path veers to the right and leads to Springbanks Arch, a small tunnel running under the road above. Springbanks Arch, a silted-over passage that leads to the North Meadow ball fields, awaits restoration as of this writing. Originally the arch and its surrounding landscape were an engineering wonder, designed with cascades and pools that channeled water under the walkway to empty over a rocky water course that flowed into the Loch. Clarence Cook, writing in his 1869 *A Description of the New York Central Park,* beheld a much different Springbanks Arch. He writes:

> The pretty cascade falls into a circular basin over a rocky wall, the clefts and crannies in which are set thick with mosses and branching ferns. . . . Here in the spring, we come to find the iris and the dog-toothed violet; and, later, the cardinal flower lightens up the shade with its splendid bloom.

Springbanks Arch, built in 1863, was also designed by Calvert Vaux and Jacob Wrey Mould. Water from a spring at the northern edge of North Meadow is carried under the bridge and into the Loch. Some of the water was diverted into Sabrina's Pool, located at the northwest abutment, which is now completely silted in. Springbanks Arch is one of the few remaining features in the park still in need of restoration.

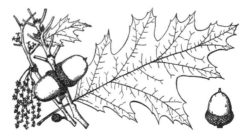

Red oak

At the beginning of the path that moves off to Springbanks Arch, two oaks stand as pillars on either side. On the left you should recognize a red oak. On the right you can examine the form and distinctive bark of a large, healthy black oak. Judging by their placement and age—easily over a hundred years old— these oaks qualify as original plantings, probably arranged by Olmsted and Vaux in this way to accent the path. About fifteen feet to the right of the black oak a young sugar maple, *Acer saccharum,* an uncommon tree in these woodlands, was planted in 1994. From the path you can identify the sugar maple by the smooth, light-colored bark and the typically palmate leaves of most maples. When it matures, the bark will roughen with vertical grooves and ridges. This particular tree was planted in the spring of 1994 as a memorial to the first woodlands crew member, Terry Clark, who died in 1993.

At the rustic bridge ahead, pause to look at the spring that gives Springbanks Arch its name. In July and August the water is reduced to a trickle, and small pools, used by birds to bathe in, often form downstream. The thicket of shrubs spread out beyond the small pools is composed mostly of the shrub arrowwood, *Viburnum dentatum,* recognized by the somewhat egg-shaped leaves with coarse teeth along the edges. The species name, *dentatum,* means toothed. The dense thicket and the sprouts from the fallen black willows offer the shelter necessary for the birds to elude most predators, which in Central Park are feral cats and hawks. Despite the cover, however, a sharp-shinned hawk, *Accipiter striatus,* a raptor of the woodlands, has been observed here taking sparrows.

The tour continues over the rustic bridge along the paved path to the left. The dirt trail moving through the trees directly ahead is a patent example of a "desire path," so named because the users of it desire to take the shortcut rather than walk the long way around on the legitimate paved path.

Desire paths are the bane of the woodlands as well as the rest of the park. An alternate and more appropriate sobriquet for these paths is "outlaw trail," because, technically, offpath use in the park breaks the rules.

On the downstream edge of the arrowwood thicket a large, fallen black willow, parallel to the path, forms a barrier between the dry land and the rivulet. Between the end of the fallen willow and the knoll with the two large trees, an unpaved, rustic access leads to the water and to another large black willow looming up in the center of a small island. A few stones direct pedestrian traffic to the water from this point, while the natural barriers—the knoll on the right and the thicket on the left—help protect the plants.

A 1994 restoration project began at the edge of the water where the oxbow channel curves around the island. This channel was dug out of the silt by volunteers working during the hot days of summer. An organic dam constructed of jute cloth and stuffed with leaves was laid from bank to bank, thirty feet downstream from the island, using wooden stakes to secure the dam in place. Over time, leaves and branches became ensnared behind the jute dam creating a more natural dam, raising the water level enough to keep the oxbow filled and the island undisturbed. Once foot traffic was curtailed, a thicket of wetland flora was planted and grew quickly in the favorable environment, providing additional cover and food for wildlife.

This and other such thickets in this ravine are the best locations from which to observe the frenzy of the spring migration that begins with the arrival of the warblers and the flowering of the red maples and trout lilies in early April and lasts until late May when the crab apples have lost their bloom. You need only position yourself anywhere along the stream with a pair of binoculars and a bird book. Because many of the migrants, especially warblers, dart quickly from spot to spot in search of insects, and are difficult to identify, beginners often refer to them as LBJs (Little Brown Jobs). Patience and a keen eye are necessary to distinguish one warbler from another. Easier to identify are mourning doves, cardinals, blue jays, woodpeckers, chickadees, mockingbirds, grackles, and the occasional red-tailed hawk, which feeds on squirrels and pigeons here. The grackles, wintering in flocks, often make their rounds through these woods, perching briefly, moving on, perching, moving on, and looking very much like black leaves blowing through the trees. The pleasures of bird-watching were not unknown to the early caretakers of the park. In the tenth annual report on Central Park in 1866 comes this observation:

> The varieties of native birds appear in their accustomed seasons at the Park, and leave on their annual migrations when the weather becomes too severe for them. Great pains are taken to secure them an unmolested habitation and to free them from annoyances and practices that are calculated to frighten them, in the hope that they will continue to add to the Park the charms of their interesting habits, their plumage, and song.

American Redstart

On the island, after the last of the spring migrants have moved north in May, the prominent blossoms of the swamp rose, *Rosa palustris,* appear. The species name, *palustris,* is from the Latin "of the swamps." The pale pink flowers of this hearty rose enhance the island through June when they give way to large, bright-red rose hips in late summer. The hips, held on purple stems, are eaten by wintering birds when snow covers other food. Two other island flowers to look for in late summer are the blue cardinal flower, *Lobelia siphilitica,* and the red cardinal flower, *Lobelia cardinalis.* The red cardinal flower attracts the Northeast's only species of hummingbird during the autumn migration.

Across the path from the fallen willow tree, a gentle slope rises through the woods toward the southeast. The plant composition on this harsh, north-facing, thin-soiled, rocky slope reflects that of the rocky woodland where patches of arrowwood and a sparse ground cover of wildflowers and woodland grasses survive. The white wood aster, *Aster divaricatus,* and several mosses dominate the vegetation here, along with scattered raspberries, ferns, and poison ivy.

The white wood aster has the distinction of being the most common wildflower in Central Park. It can be identified from August to the first frost of autumn by the flat-topped clusters of petite, daisylike white flowers, each with eight to twelve ray petals and yellow centers that turn purple by October. The aster's dark, zigzag stem and elongated, heart-shaped leaves were used by Native Americans as a potherb to flavor their cooking. Half a dozen other aster species are found throughout the woodlands, but only the white wood aster is tenacious enough to grow from the cracks in rocks and from soil that has the consistency of concrete. If not for its beauty, its usefulness in erosion control, and the fact that it is a self-seeding native plant, it would be considered a weed, as it is in some suburban gardens. But what is a weed but a plant that someone doesn't want?

On the same slope in the first and second weeks of April, trout lily, *Erythronium americanum,* a springtime ephemeral, appears for two weeks then returns to the soil until the following April. Trout lily has typical lily flowers: bell-shaped, four to ten inches high, with six petals on a nodding inflorescence that becomes a small berrylike fruit before the entire plant goes dormant again. Its common name, trout lily, comes from the two mottled green leaves that resemble the skin of some fanciful trout. Because of its moist spring soil, this slope is home to the largest colony of trout lilies in the park.

On the left past the fallen willow, about twenty feet up on a knoll, two majestic trees spread out into the canopy. The tree on the right is a red oak, identified by the ski trails on the upper bark and by its typical oak leaves. The other is an American elm, *Ulmus americana,* found in its natural habitat growing in bottomlands near rivers and in moist places, as this one is. The seeds of American elms are eaten by numerous animals, most of which are not found in the park. Nevertheless, if you stand under an American elm in April and May you will notice a litter of seed casings emptied by squirrels who savor the seeds. Large elms are becoming less common in the Northeast. Since the early twentieth century they have become plagued by Dutch elm disease, a pernicious and deadly fungus, explained at length on the Harlem Meer Walk.

Farther ahead a rustic rail begins on the right side of the path in a thicket of arrowwood. The logs used to construct the rail were collected from Pelham Bay Park in the Bronx after a powerful storm in 1992 tore through, leveling over a thousand black locusts. The wood of these trees resists rot so well that hundred-year-old black locust fences still stand in the nearby countryside. The serpentine rail, whose undulations appear to slither along its path, was installed to prevent bike riders from crossing between the meadow and the woodlands.

Farther along the path on the right the trunks of three European white birches, *Betula pendula*—two alive, one dead at this writing—remain from a planting done in the 1930s. An examination of their leaves distinguishes them from the American paper birch, *Betula papyrifera*. The European birch leaves are

Paper birch

more diamond-shaped, whereas the American birches' leaves are more oval-shaped. Birches grow exclusively in the Northern Hemisphere. As pioneer trees, they are short-lived and decline after fifty or sixty years, dropping limbs and twigs until they topple completely. These particular trees were planted to be seen from the top of the meadow where their unmistakable white bark and stiff form contrast with the soft form and yellowish hue of the black willows that grow along the Loch.

Looking beyond the birches, a wildflower meadow stretches skyward from the wooded Ravine, extending up the north-facing slope from the Loch to the road connecting the East and West Drives. The native grasses and wildflowers purchased for the meadow were donated in large part by the Garden Club of America, although the meadow should not be mistaken for a garden. Preparation and planting of the meadow was begun in the spring of 1994 and continues as of this writing.

A plant list and map of Central Park, compiled in 1873 by landscape architect Robert Demcker, indicates that this area was a meadow even then. The Demcker list documents the vegetation in the woodlands surrounding the meadow but includes names of only a few wildflower species in the meadow itself—early saxifrage, mayapple, plume poppy, and a number of asters. Only the asters have survived into this century, mingled with goldenrod and many less colorful weeds.

From the first week of July and continuing well into autumn, dazzling colors and wildlife activity enchant visitors in the meadow. *Rudbeckia* species thrive here, including the coneflowers and black-eyed Susan, with their bright and various yellow, purple, and orange daisylike blossoms, which last throughout the summer. In late summer and well into autumn some other strong performers bring luster to the meadow: bee balm, *Monarda didyma,* attracts hummingbirds and butterflies with its bright red flowers and minty fragrance; New England aster, *Aster novae-angliae,* dazzles with its clusters of pastel-like blue starry flowers well into November; white snakeroot, *Eupatorium alba,* offers small billowy clusters of long lasting inflorescence; Canadian goldenrod, *Solidago canadensis,* has six-foot-tall wands of lemon yellow stature, thick canes that are a stable perch for many bird species foraging the meadow for insects and seeds; cup-plant, *Silphium perfoliatum,* a tall sunflowerlike western prairie plant whose cupped leaves hold water and provide seeds that are relished by many birds.

Since the meadow's inception, many species of butterflies, birds, and pollinating insects have been spotted foraging in the showy stands of flowers and grasses. In the autumn of 1994 the Leconte's sparrow, *Passerherbulus caudacutus,* a bird of the western prairie, visited the meadow, the first time that the species was ever recorded in Central Park. That same autumn several pairs of recently rare bluebirds, *Sialia sialis,* declared the State Bird of New York by Governor Nelson Rockefeller in 1970, paused to rest and feed here while migrating south. The bluebirds and their habitat have been greatly reduced in southern New York, displaced by land development and European birds, such as the starling and the European house sparrow, which, because of their overabundance and aggressiveness, have won the best nesting sites. Other wildlife spotted in this meadow include warblers, titmice, phoebes, kingbirds, hummingbirds, chickadees, several finch and sparrow species, red-tailed hawks, rabbits, and field mice.

Along the edge of the meadow, look for the several shrubs and vines planted for wildlife food and cover as well as for their aesthetics. These include shadbush, elderberry, bayberry, shrub dogwood, arrowwood, blackberry, trumpetvine, and honeysuckle.

Shadbush

Return to the path and follow the sound of water rushing over the third cascade farther ahead. On the left, before the path diverges to the right, a small hemlock, *Tsuga canadensis,*

Hemlock

stands in front of a large, fallen black willow trunk. Hemlocks are easily identified by their soft evergreen needles with silvery undersides. The 1982 tree survey lists only nineteen hemlocks over six inches in diameter. In the wild, hemlocks attain heights over 100 feet, but Central Park's dry soil, stress, and pollution make that height unlikely. Most of the hemlocks in the park are infected with woolly adelgid, a tiny aphidlike insect that sucks the sap out of the hemlock's branchlets. The adelgid has been spreading among the eastern hemlocks since the 1970s. The tiny insects are easily checked with applications of a nontoxic insecticidal oil that smothers them. Unfortunately, the oil must be applied tree by tree, which is not feasible in densely populated parks or in a forested environment. The infestation is spreading north and could wipe out one of the Northeast's best-loved conifers.

A springtime witch hazel, *Hamamelis vernalis,* recognized by its large, wavy leaves and dense shrubby form, grows at the end of the willow trunk near the edge of the steep slope overlooking the cascade. This witch hazel produces many small, fragrant yellow to reddish flowers from January to April, thus the species name, *vernalis,* for spring. The seeds, twigs, and buds of witch hazel provide food for many species of wildlife and is also the same shrub that provides rubbing liniment for sprains and bruises.

The path separates up ahead with one path branching to the right. Continue straight down the incline a few feet to another narrow bluestone path off to the right curving through the thick vegetation. This single-file path was installed as part of an erosion-control project and came to be known as the Indian Path because it moves people single-file through the woods, much the same as Native Americans traveled. A diversity of small trees, shrubs, and wildflowers are encountered along this path. In late summer and into autumn the ground is thick with asters and snakeroot. Young tulip trees dominate, recognized by light-gray bark speckled with small white blotches and their unique four-pointed, notched leaves. The spindly shrub growing from the knoll on the right at the entrance to the Indian Path is sweet pepperbush, which was also encountered on the rocky slope at Glen Span Bridge.

Back on the path and down the slight incline, a three-boulder bridge crosses the water on the left. Before crossing that bridge we'll examine Huddlestone Arch, down the path to the right. In his 1990 book, *The Bridges of Central Park,* Henry Hope Reed says of this bridge:

> Of all the archways in Central Park, Huddlestone is the most picturesque. To sit at Huddlestone's southern portal on a spring day in the Ravine is not to be in New York, but in a country setting where forsythia abounds and the sound of a gently flowing brook soothes the spirit.

The forsythia Reed mentions drapes over the entrance to the arch from the roadway above and, in March, a cascade of yellow blossoms spills over the top of the arch along its viny stems.

Beneath Huddlestone and across the water from the path, a mammoth boulder dips into the stream, fancifully resembling a dinosaur sipping from the stream. The Central Park *Annual Report of 1866* cites the moving of many boulders for the construction of Huddlestone Arch and estimates one boulder, this dinosaur, at one hundred tons.

On the other side of Huddlestone is the Lula B. Lasker Swimming Pool and Skating Rink and parking lot, erected in the 1960s. Before the imposition of this architecturally bland structure, there was a pleasant change between the two landscapes framed by Huddlestone Arch. Where Lasker Rink now stands, old photographs depict a rustic bridge crossing the rivulet before it emptied into the Harlem Meer, providing a

wide vista that opened out onto the broad waters of the Meer
beyond. It is unfortunate that we've lost that artfully designed
vista, which complemented the transition from the woodlands
to the Harlem Meer.

Return to the path that leads across the three-boulder
bridge. Before crossing the bridge, examine the natural spring
tucked into the boulders on the left. In springtime and late
autumn, the spring is filled with water seeping in from the
water table located to the south at North Meadow. This
spring and several others throughout the park supplied drinking water to park users until the turn of the century. An eye-
bolt can be seen on the left side of the boulder above the
spring; it held a ladle used to dip into the spring. The drinking ladle was excavated during restoration of the Huddlestone area in 1991 and is now on display at the Dana
Learning Center, which we'll visit on the Harlem Meer Walk.
Through much of the year, the spring is dry, in part because
most of the groundwater is channeled out of the park and
into the Ward's Island treatment plant through over a hundred miles of drainage pipes below ground. However, even
when the spring is full, it is not advisable to drink the water
because the pollution levels of Manhattan's groundwater
vary considerably.

Across the three-boulder bridge, at the foot of the stairs
and immediately on the right, another majestic but declining
red oak looms up and leans slightly over the water to meet the
large red oak on the opposite bank. The positioning and age,
well over a hundred years, of these two oaks qualify them as
original plantings.

On the other side of the red snow fence farther up the
slope, an ambitious ecological restoration is taking place. In
1990, this slope was an eroded nexus of desire paths and
trampled vegetation. With the help of volunteers, much of the
slope was stabilized with cribbing logs, amended soil, and

hundreds of yards of leaf litter and jute mesh, an erosion-control fabric woven from the fibers of the jute plant, an Asian herb of the linden tree family. This kind of maintenance and restoration in Central Park's woodlands focuses on the ecological health of the area rather than on cosmetics alone. Although aesthetics are an important ingredient in the work performed—wildflowers, rustic structures, cascades, etc.—the impetus comes from the health of the forest rather than from the eye of the beholder.

The practicality of ecological restoration has been proven time and again across America and the world. Awareness of the problems in the environment is now widespread, yet solutions are slow in coming. William K. Stevens dedicates an entire book, *Miracle Under the Oaks,* to a grass-roots restoration effort that reclaimed a shattered prairie-savanna remnant ecosystem along the Chicago River in the suburbs of Chicago. Stevens explains its goal and purposes:

> The express and primary goal is to preserve and promote biological diversity and the relationships among organisms, earth, air, sunlight, and water that ecologists call "ecosystem functions.". . . The purpose is to recreate as nearly as possible the essentials of the ecosystem's structure, including as many original species of plants, animals, and microbes as possible, and enable them to interact as they once did.
>
> Restoration is gardening in a sense, and also agriculture, but what a big difference: Its purpose is not to shape nature to one's aesthetic taste or to make a living, but rather to enable nature to take its own course. It seeks not to control and modify natural processes, but free them. It places humans not above the rest of nature, but in it, and not just as an admirer but as a participant.

Many different plant species common in the oak-hickory forest now occupy the slope on the other side of the red-snow fence. Park woodsmen monitor the health of such species as mountain laurel, *Kalmia latifolia,* found growing in rocky

Mountain laurel

woods like these and recognizable because of its evergreen foliage and, in June, its delicate, clustered white-purple flowers; stands of mapleleaf viburnum, *Viburnum acerifolium,* a shrub with distinctively maple-shaped leaves; flowering dogwood, *Cornus florida,* most evident in early May when in flower; and a variety of ferns and a diversity of woodland wildflowers such as Solomon's plume, wild geranium, baneberry, and jack-in-the-pulpit. The fence, to be maintained indefinitely, creates a kind of reversed woodland zoo, keeping the observed safe from the observer.

At the top of the stairs, a stately sweet gum, *Liquidambar styraciflua,* another woodland favorite, enhances the stature of oaks and a tulip tree with its broad bole, widespread crown, and grayish, grooved bark pattern. This mature sweet gum may have originally been planted with the oaks and tulip tree to form a majestic stand of trees to accent the stairs and cascade.

Ahead on the right are a series of dilapidated stairs that once connected this path to another path up the slope. To the left of the stairs, look for a large black oak, a healthy specimen, growing from a rock outcrop.

At this point in the walk the stream flows far below the path, presenting another opportunity for viewing wildlife activity. Many of the park's more than two hundred species of birds congregate in the wet thicket below. This is, in a sense, a hawk's-eye view and not unknown to the red-tailed hawks that can sometimes be seen swooping through the trees to take a pigeon or rabbit from the edge of the thicket along the rivulet. From this vantage point, where visitors are at eye level with the tree canopy, many of the canopy-dwelling species, especially the elusive warblers, are more accessible to bird-watchers.

Farther along this slope, between the path that veers to the right and the rustic bridge up ahead, a diversity of woodland wildflowers were planted. They include columbine, *Aquilegia canadensis,* recognized by the upside-down red flower with yellow center that blooms in May and June; Allegheny spurge, *Pachysandra procumbens,* a low evergreen ground cover displaying pinkish white flowers in early April; woodland goldenrod, *Solidago caesia,* a typical slender goldenrod, one to three feet high with yellow flower tufts tucked into the stem in August and September; alumroot, *Heuchera americana;* jack-in-the-pulpit, *Arisaema atrorubens,* another early spring bloom with an unusual flower similar to skunk cabbage; wild geranium, *Geranium maculatum;* and the dominant flower of this area, the white wood aster, *Aster divaricatus,* in autumn.

Just off the path on the left farther along, a small stand of American beech, *Fagus grandifolia,* has formed a typical beech grove. American beeches can be recognized by their smooth gray bark, looking much like pale elephant's hide, and by their elliptical, coarse-toothed leaves. All but two of the smaller beeches are sprouts from the large tree's roots. Beeches typically multiply this way, allowing them to surge upward and enter the canopy as the large trees decline. Notice that nothing grows

American beech

within this stand of trees other than the beeches themselves. This is typical of how beech forests grow, with only a few scattered seedlings beneath the beech. Between November and March their dead leaves cling to the branches, until spring, when the beeches' pale rust color projects against the gray bark and their sound in the wind rustles the solitude of the winter woods.

Across the path from the beeches, a large boulder invites strollers to rest on its flat ledge. Move on past the boulder and look for another hemlock up the slope on the right, which is about the same size as the hemlock at the Huddlestone cascade and was possibly planted at the same time. Forty feet beyond the hemlock another large black oak leans over the edge of the path. The top of the tree was removed for safety's sake after a severe winter storm in 1992 cracked the base of the tree. If you stand facing the oak from the path, you can examine the scar of the fissure at its base on the lower left.

Across the path from the oak a medium-size ironwood, *Carpinus* sp., twists twenty feet into the trees. The ironwood's smooth, rippled, steel-gray bark suggests its other common name, musclewood. In the wild, this tree would be found growing in these same conditions, in bottomlands where the slope levels out as it approaches a stream, collecting moisture and rich alluvial soil.

Continue along past the black oak and ironwood for about thirty feet. Spreading out low on the right, a patch of poison ivy, *Rhus radicans,* deters visitors to the woodlands from wandering off the path. Poison ivy is best identified by its three leaves on a short stem and, contrary to popular belief, only its young leaves are shiny—they become dull with age in late summer.

The crimson foliage of poison ivy contends with the sugar maples for colorful autumnal displays in this area. Although poisonous to humans, the berries are enjoyed by at least sixty species of birds, which helps the plant spread rapidly. Poison ivy is a dominant plant, close by ocean beaches along the Eastern Seaboard. In other areas of the park poison ivy is removed with herbicide, but in the woodlands, where it is both an indicator of the native woods and beneficial to wildlife, it remains to fill its particular niche. If more people were aware of its existence in the park, they would stay on the path.

The path curves slightly up ahead and leads to the third rustic bridge. From the bridge, the last tree to identify is the river birch, *Betula nigra,* seen on the left looming up from the knoll and leaning out over the cascade. The 1982 survey lists 82 river birches in the park. The dark, patchy, rough bark of this species distinguishes it from the white birches seen near the meadow. This specimen was placed on the knoll to grow prominently over the cascade. River birches are our largest and longest-lived birches, growing in low woods near streams and rivers with other riverine forest species such as black willow, American elm, pin oak, pepperbush, woodbine, and poison ivy, which have all been seen on this tour.

The tour ends here with the sound of cascading water, a deep view of an urban woodland, and this quote from Andrew H. Green, an original Central Park Commissioner who argued for an arboretum to be located in Central Park in 1862:

The forests of the country, with their magnificent beauties, the growth of centuries, are being swept away rapidly and wastefully, and the beasts and the birds that live in their shelter are becoming extinct for want of an intelligent appreciation of their value, both to the present and coming generations.

Meer Walk

Harlem Meer,
5th Avenue at 106th Street

THIS WALK BEGINS at Fifth Avenue and 106th Street. Along the way we will pass by the remnant of a mountain, through a transformed marsh, and through an ancient plain. The tour includes two forts dating back to the Revolutionary War and the foundation relic of a nineteenth-century convent, a tavern, and a sculpture museum.

Before entering the park take a moment to admire the elm trees shading Fifth Avenue from 110th Street as far south as the eye can see. These trees are the longest contiguous stand of American elms in the world. They stretch branch to branch from 110th Street to 59th Street, a distance of two and a half miles, interrupted only briefly at the Metropolitan Museum of Art. *The 1982 Tree Inventory* lists over 1,800 American elms in the park, 12 percent of all the park's 26,000 trees, with half of those elms growing along Fifth Avenue. That Dutch elm disease has not killed more elms in the park is a compliment to Central Park's arboriculturists, who search the canopy of each individual elm from May through July for signs of the disease.

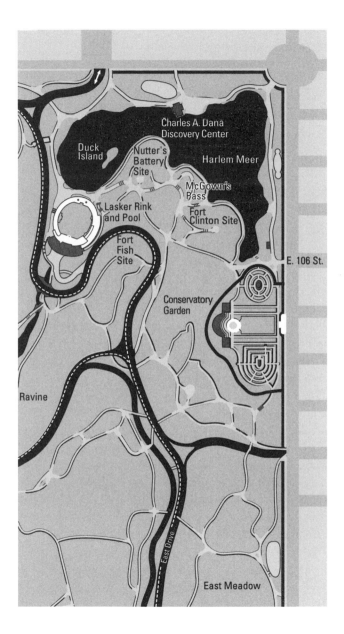

Charles A. Dana
Discovery Center

Duck
Island

Nutter's
Battery
Site

Harlem Meer

McGown's
Pass

Lasker Rink
and Pool

Fort
Clinton Site

Fort
Fish
Site

E. 106 St.

Conservatory
Garden

Ravine

East Drive

East Meadow

When found, they prevent it from spreading into the roots where it can infect neighboring elms.

American elm

Dutch elm disease, caused by the fungus *Ceratocystis ulmi,* came to America from the Netherlands in 1930. Since then it has killed over half of the American elms on this continent. Even with diligent surveillance, the elms in the park still succumb at the rate of about 1 percent a year. After removing infected trees that cannot be saved, young elms are usually planted in their place.

Enter the park and follow the pipe rail around to the water fountain. A well-placed stand of about a dozen trees forms a grove here that spreads out along the path between the wall and the water. As we step into this open grove of large trees, coming from the rigid monolith of buildings on Fifth Avenue, we are especially grateful to have Central Park. Even with the rumblings of traffic on the other side of the wall, this grove transports us out of the urban cacophony and into a quieter realm, much as a trip to the country would.

The first three trees in the grove, two on the left and one on the right, are red oaks, *Quercus rubra.* All are about the same size and serve as portals to the Harlem Meer landscape. The red oaks can be recognized by the typical oak leaf and smooth gray bark, with lines like ski trails running down from the top two-thirds of the crown. Up ahead, a horse chestnut, *Aesculus hippocastanum,* with its arching branches and dense rounded crown, softens the bland architecture of the redbrick concession building on the left. Horse chestnuts were a popular landscape tree for Frederick Olmsted and Calvert Vaux. One of the park's original horse chestnut plantings is encountered on the 100th Street Pool Walk. The horse chestnut makes an interesting all-season landscape tree because of its attractive curved branching pattern in winter, the light-gray somewhat flaky bark, the showy spires of white flowers in May, the distinctive fan-shaped, seven-blade leaves in summer, and the thorny husks of yellow-green fruit in autumn. A smaller horse chestnut thrives alongside the larger one, primed to be its replacement after the older tree dies and is removed, but maybe not for another hundred years.

Moving through the grove some other trees are worth noting. On the right, across from the horse chestnuts, four large turkey oaks, *Quercus cerris,* rise up statuesquely with their dark plated bark and angular crowns. Half of all turkey oaks in the park are found around the reservoir and will be discussed on that tour. Back on the other side of the path a European beech, *Fagus sylvatica,* can be recognized by its smooth gray bark, five main trunks, and a base that fancifully resembles a giant elephant's foot. Judging by its size and slow growth, this beech may be an original planting. The genus name *Fagus* originates from the Greek *phagein,* to eat. The nuts were once fed to pigs and were also a favorite food of passenger pigeons and Carolina parakeets, both of which became extinct early in the the twentieth century. Now squirrels relish the nuts, as do a number of migratory birds and such residents as blue jays, titmice, grosbeaks, nuthatches, and several species of woodpeckers.

Behind the European beech, two bald cypresses, *Taxodium distichum,* are recognized by their deciduous green needles clustered along green twigs and by their distinctive reddish brown, fibrous bark. (Another bald cypress of equal stature is encountered and discussed in the 100th Street Pool Walk.) The towering figures of these trees, seen clearly from the far banks of the Meer, accentuate the landscape on this southeastern edge of the water. Before leaving, keep in mind that cypresses lose their needles in winter, at which time they look like dead spruces.

It's unusual to find a beech tree growing side by side with cypress trees. Each tree prefers starkly different habitats, the beech thriving in dry upland conditions, while the cypress requires swampy conditions. Too much water will send a beech into decline and an early death, and too little water will stunt the bald cypress, if not kill it. Before the park was built and the city reached this far north, a tidal marsh spread out from here to the East River; it was filled in during the northernly advance of the city. A high water table still exists not far from the surface, allowing moisture-loving flora such as the cypress to thrive. Yet, because the ground is filled in with dry soil above the water table, shallow rooted, upland flora, such as the beech, can also thrive. It should be noted that the Harlem Meer, at about this point, is the lowest spot in the park, at five feet above sea level. The highest point is Summit Rock, rising 137 feet above Central Park West inside the wall at 83rd Street.

A black willow, *Salix nigra,* past the beech on the left, is the final tree to examine in this grove, recognized by its slender, linear leaves, dark furrowed bark, and bushy habit of the crown. Large stands of black willows are encountered on the Loch tour. Willow species along the Northeast's coast are synonymous with water, though a large number of willow species grow high and dry on the windswept tundra from Alaska to Newfoundland. Many of the tundra species grow to only a few inches in height and resemble exotic terrarium plants more

Black willow

than our common northeastern willows. On the tundra, where vegetation is sparse, the buds, leaves, and fruits of the small willows feed the ptarmigans, elk, moose, rabbits, and other animals that inhabit that formidable environment. In Central Park, willows provide abundant insects and perches for birds above the waterways. Their bark once provided tannin for making leather and ink, and salicin, the basic ingredient in aspirin. Gray's *Manual of Botany* lists over fifty species of willow with the taxonomic caveat that they freely hybridize.

Moving out of the grove, a miniature beach will be encountered at the water's edge. The beach was designed as a landscape feature for this large body of water, not for swimming. Nevertheless, on the first hot summer days after completion of the Harlem Meer restoration in 1994, many residents of the community couldn't resist the water's allure. Unfortunately, the water is shallow and the bottom a muddy quagmire, which makes it potentially hazardous to bathers. Since it wasn't cost effective to redesign the beach into turf or a rocky edge, park managers compromised with the public by allowing wading out to a barrier fence, which is posted with a DANGER sign.

Across the southern edge of the water, cliffs rise from the shore to the landscape high above. In 1858, the park terminated at 106th Street, in line with those cliffs. The first park commissioners sagely convinced the city government to acquire the rough and craggy land and marshes north to 110th Street. The land was purchased and added to the park in 1863, bringing the park's estate from 624 acres to its present 843 acres.

No design existed for the marshy land or the Harlem Creek and marsh that ran through it. Early descriptions and maps in the annual reports propose that a formal canal was to be constructed connecting the park to the East River. That plan was soon abandoned for a more economical one that created the North Lake, which later became the Harlem Lake, today's Harlem "Meer," from the Dutch word for lake, which in turn derived from a Greek word for sea. Excavation of the 12-plus acres of the Meer yielded more than 200,000 cubic yards of sand and gravel. The material was used to fill in unwanted swamps and marshes and to raise low spots throughout the park. Ten thousand cubic yards of the Meer excavation went to the East Meadow between 101st and 97th Streets along Fifth Avenue.

On the north edge of the water, the Dana Discovery Center rises, like the phoenix, from the restored landscape. A restaurant erected in 1966 on the same site was burned beyond restoration twenty years later and stood in ruins until 1992, when restoration of the Meer began. The Central Park Conservancy, the Dana Foundation, the Lila Wallace-Reader's Digest Fund, and the Cissy Patterson Trust joined together to finance the $16 million restoration, which was completed in 1994. The result is the pleasant lake that is the subject of this tour.

Before restoration, the area was used primarily by dog walkers, a few fishermen, and some unsavory characters who gave the north end of the park a bad reputation. Today a crew of Harlem Meer zone gardeners, the backbone of the Meer's restoration, sweeps, paints, rakes, and cleans the playgrounds and water. Zone gardeners work within a maintenance system instituted in the early 1990s that divides the park into sections and zones, and an important aspect of their work is their ability to listen and interact with the community, which in turn contributes to the sense of community stewardship necessary to maintain a healthy Central Park.

Opposite the beach, near the perimeter wall, five young white pines, *Pinus strobus,* the second most common pine in the park after the Austrian pine, *Pinus nigra,* can be recognized by their evergreen needles, clustered five to a bundle, the only pine with five needles. The white pine is the most important tree in the Northeast's lumber industry. Its forests once extended from Maine south to the Carolinas, but white pine has been lumbered so extensively that no virgin stands of it survive today. Only a few trees more than a century old can be found in the wild today and those only in state parks. White pines grow quickly, often as a pioneer species after forest fires. They easily attain heights over a hundred feet in their mountainous habitat, and specimens over two hundred feet have been recorded, though such trees no longer exist. Today white pine is found scattered throughout the Northeast, but most abundantly in New England.

White pine

Up ahead on the right, a restored playground, donated by the Bernard family, opened, to the delight of many children and parents, in 1991 before the entire Meer restoration was completed. Several stunning trees and some ground cover enhance the swings, slides, sandboxes, and surrounding area, including several dignified ginkgoes. One tree not yet encoun-

American linden

tered on these walks is the stately, little-leaved linden, *Tilia cordata,* inside the gate to the left. It is recognized by its sweeping form and slightly lopsided, heart-shaped leaves. During the second week of June, the powerfully sweet fragrance of the tiny, inconspicuous flowers of this and other linden species is evidenced nearly everywhere in the park. Five species of linden are found in the park, amounting to nearly seven hundred individual trees, though only the American linden, *Tilia americana,* is native to this continent. It is distinguished from the others by its large leaves, which can grow to a diameter of eight inches. The leaves of the other lindens, of European and Asian origin, are only two to four inches across. However, American lindens cannot tolerate pollution as well as the alien species and survive only a few years on the city streets.

Along the Meer's eastern edge, in the water, spires of blue flowers on the pickerel weed, *Pontederia cordata,* rise up from large arrow-shaped leaves during the second week of July and last through August. Pickerel weed grows in the same habitat as the pickerel fish, *Esox niger,* in quiet lakes and ponds, although no pickerel are found in this body of water. The fruit pods of pickerel weed are small bulbs with many starchy seeds. Several duck species favor these seeds and, according to some sources, roasted seeds were used for cereals and breads by Native Americans. The genus name *Pontederia* is a dedication by Linnaeus to Guilio Pontedera (d. 1756), a renowned professor who taught in Padua, Italy.

In hot summer months you may notice bubbles rising to the surface of the water in different locations. The bubbles come from aerators (perforated tubes running from Lasker Rink along the bottom of the Meer), which help to oxygenate the water. The aerators mix the water and increase oxygen levels available to the fish. At its deepest the Meer is eight feet, close by the Dana Center's portico, but the average depth is about four feet. Only fish tolerant of low dissolved oxygen levels do well here. The aeration system compensates for the warm, shallow water, which by nature has low oxygen levels.

Compounding the problem of shallow, still water in the Meer is the overabundance of algae. The summer algal blooms are often so thick that the water cannot be seen. The algae thrive, supported by the nutrients from fertilizers washed into the water from surrounding landscapes and by an abundance of sunlight that penetrates to the bottom of the shallow water. Yet, even with the aerators, fish kills may occur during extended sultry periods in the summer because the dense algae consume most of the limited oxygen.

Asian grass carp have been added to feed on the algae, but they are restricted in number by the Department of Environmental Conservation (DEC). If successful, the carp will reduce the algae population, keep the water more open to floral diversity, cool the water, and reduce the potential for fish kills in midsummer. Also, carp are bottom feeders, which will keep the water muddied and reduce light penetration to the bottom where the algae grow, and thus slow algal growth.

Follow the path around to the left past Pioneer's Gate, which is the park entrance at 110th Street and Fifth Avenue. Surrounding the entrance are the first of the elms stretching contiguously south to 59th Street. The elms and a few other species around them appear weakened by two years of construction of the surrounding landscape. From 1992 to 1994, the trees' root systems were affected when old pathways were torn up to make way for new ones. As the years take their toll on the modified landscape, so the restoration of the landscape takes its toll on the trees and shrubs. Beyond construction disturbance, the elms survived three droughts in five years, from 1992 to 1996, as well as the constant threat of Dutch elm disease. Despite the obstacles, most of these trees will recover and live many more years.

Across the path from lamppost #0906-A, two young bald cypresses introduce a wetland planting begun in 1994 that also includes red maple; witch alder, *Fothergilla gardeni;* and northern bayberry, *Myrica pensylvanica.* Red maples are recognized by their typical maple leaf and smooth bark. Witch alder, a low wetland shrub no more than three feet high, in late April has clusters of fragrant whitish blossoms before the foliage appears with small leaves resembling witch hazel, to which it is related. Witch alder's native habitat along streamsides extends from Virginia, south and west to Alabama. Its botanical name honors two distinguished gentlemen of the eighteenth century: John Fothergill, a British botanist, and Alexander Garden, the botanist who discovered the plant in its native habitat.

Bayberry is distinguished by its wedge-shaped, leathery, occasionally evergreen leaves and small white flowers clustered along the stems in June that become pale blue fruits in autumn. It is not typically a wetland plant, but grows abundantly along Long Island's sandy, barren coast as well as in meadows and throughout most of the Northeast in poor, sandy soil. A mature bayberry can reach 35 feet, but more commonly they grow to a height of six or eight feet. They are able to grow in barren soil because of their ability to "fix nitrogen." Some species of plants, most notably plants of the pea family, *Leguminosae* (black locust, honey locust, Sophora, and clover in Central Park), convert nitrogen from the atmosphere and "fix" (introduce) it into the soil.

Besides the *Leguminosae,* which includes some 13,000 species, about 300 other plant species have adapted to convert gaseous atmospheric nitrogen into a usable chemical form. Unlike bayberry, most cash crops, cereals in particular, cannot fix nitrogen and depend upon millions of dollars' worth of nitrogen fertilizer. Scientists, using recombinant DNA experiments, are attempting to introduce the nitrogen-fixing gene of the *Leguminosae* into the grain gene. In 1981 the U.S. Department of Agriculture successfully combined a French bean's seed-making gene with a sunflower cell. So far no plants have developed from the cell.

Another advantage of having bayberry in the park is its attraction to wildlife that favor its small, waxy fruit. Tree swallows, *Tachycineta bicolor,* mostly insect eaters, consume bayberries during their winter migration. More notably, the myrtle warbler, *Dendrofca coronata,* also known as the yellow-rumped warbler, will winter over in places where bayberry, poison ivy berries, and the fruits of the red cedar are abundant. The introduction of bayberry and cedar could entice more of these berry-loving species to be winter residents in Central Park.

From lamppost #0906-A, take the stony path along the water to the Dana Center and enjoy the grand view across the Meer where the bluffs on the far side cascade down to the level of the water. Imagine it before European settlers arrived and changed the conditions of Manhattan Island. Wild turkey, whitetail deer, ruffed grouse, and beaver could be found here then. Black bears, wolves, fox, and bobcats drank from the creek, which was shaded by red maple and tupelo. The iridescently patterned wood ducks nested in the cavities of trees along the shore. Herons, sandpipers, and kingfishers fed on an abundance of fish, crustaceans, and frogs in and around the creek and marsh. Interlaced with the trees, shrubs, and wildlife were colorful displays of blazing red trumpet creeper, subtle orange jewel weed, pink and white turtlehead, the starry yellow of abundant cowslips, marsh blue violets, and the bright red of the cardinal flowers, made all the more stunning by the presence of hummingbirds, finches, warblers, and bluebirds. A variety of river grapes, blueberries, and shagbark hickory nuts were available as food. Today, except for the large mammals, much of the same flora and fauna still survive along the Loch/Meer stream corridor, though much of it has been replanted in recent years. A park, like a zoo, can only hint at the pre-Columbian diversity that existed in the forests here.

With that in mind continue on to the Dana Center, which officially opened in 1993. The display room, overlooking the water, exhibits rotating displays of a variety of community artwork and projects. In the anteroom, where a staff member is ready to answer questions or give directions, many relics from the park's past are exhibited, most of them unearthed during recent restorations of the park's landscapes. Some of the items—old beer and elixir bottles, utensils, etc.—were yesterday's trash. More interesting are the tools used to build the park: picks, feather wedges used to split boulders, chisels, and other tools necessary for reshaping the rocky terrain into Central Park.

Outside the Dana Center, head west with the playground on your right. From here, as you continue west, scan the far bank and horizon to see some attractive and distracting landscape and architectural effects. Directly across from the playground a rock-studded promontory pinches the Meer to its narrowest point. Atop the promontory stood Nutter's Battery, one of a series of three nearby forts used by the British during the Revolutionary War. Off to the left, the round-topped, red-trimmed Terence Cardinal Cooke Hospital complements the design of the Dana Center. To the right of the promontory, Duck Island was constructed to replace an island destroyed by the construction of Lasker Rink, which we'll examine later.

An imposing group of some twenty black locust trees stands on the extreme western bank of the Meer. From the last week of May through the first two weeks of June bright white flowers cover the crowns of these trees, which shimmer in the blue sky. This is arguably the finest stand of black locusts in the park, overwhelming passersby with the honey-scented fragrance of its blossoms. From a list compiled in 1873 by landscape architect Robert Demcker, we know that this western edge of the Meer was planted with green alder, mock orange, box honeysuckle, and Scotch elm. Over the years those plants died out and, judging by their size, this group of locust trees was planted in the 1920s or 1930s. They create a stunning landscape effect in or out of flower.

Off to the right, across the East Drive, the true woodlands rise up the steep slope. If it's a pleasant weekend afternoon and many people are picnicking in the park and playing near the water on the closely cropped turf, the contrast of light and sound between the bustling Meer and the hushed woodlands is almost eerie. Only occasionally are strollers seen moving along the woodland paths, even as activity abounds around the Meer. The allure of the wooded serenity is restrained by our wariness of its isolation. An enjoyable side tour through these woods will take you over historic trails to the oldest structure in the park, the Block House. However, as with any isolated place in the city, keep your street smarts about you.

Even though crime has decreased in the park by over 40 percent, compared to the 1970s, the potential for danger remains. Bear the isolation factor in mind and enjoy these secluded areas with a friend.

On the other side of the stand of locusts the path to the right leads to Lasker Rink. Built in the 1950s, the rink accommodates ice skaters in winter and swimmers in summer. The rink and pool offer recreation to thousands of New York City residents each year. Unfortunately the rink did not get the scrutiny that park structures of such magnitude deserve. Architecturally, Lasker Rink clashes with the Olmstedian structures in the park (compare it to the grand Victorian design of the Dana Center or the Dairy at the lower end of the park). Lasker Rink's austere lines and gross display of concrete give it more the appearance of a fortress than a recreation center. It was also badly engineered, built over the outflow of the Loch, the stream that feeds the Meer. The unstable wet ground has caused the structure to shift and leak, resulting in repair costs of thousands of dollars.

Where Lasker now stands an island once rose out of the Meer, which was designed to resemble a delta island at the mouth of a river, tapered by the flow of water from the Loch. The island was scraped away to make way for the rink. During restoration of the Meer, a new island was added, seen to

Pitch pine

the east. It was appropriately named Duck Island, as water-fowl frequent the site and mallard ducks and swans nest there. Native flora were planted on the island and quickly formed a dense thicket that attracted an array of wildlife. The thicket is composed in part of pitch pine, *Pinus rigida,* which can grow to fifty feet; bayberry, seen earlier around the Dana Center; joe-pye weed, *Eupatorium purpureum,* with fuzzy clusters of pinkish purple blossoms in late July; pickerel weed, seen along the eastern shore of the Meer; and a number of grasses, including some aggressive alien species, which were seeded by wind and birds.

This vegetation forms an isolated thicket protected by the water and the black pipe rail that encircles the island to keep rowboats from landing. In the winter, if the water freezes, cottontail rabbits, *Sylvilagus floridanus,* cross the ice and feed on the twigs and buds. Rarely seen in the park because they are somewhat nocturnal, rabbits occupy the edges between woods and meadows, known as an ecotone to ecologists. Rabbits do not hibernate, so in winter, when less cover is available to them, you might see a red-tailed hawk, *Buteo jamaicensis,* at least two of which are year-round park residents, feeding on a rabbit. But don't be too concerned for cottontails, which live for five or six years and breed after nine months of age, producing several litters a year. In his *Complete Field Guide to American Wildlife,* Henry Hill Collins, Jr., observes that rabbits "have been extraordinarily successful animals during the last fifty or sixty million years. From the evolutionary view point these mammals represent in many respects the climax of mammalian success."

The path diverges at lamppost #0750. Take the high road up the steps leading to Nutter's Battery. At the top of the steps at lamppost #0736, take the path left into the stone circle. Nutter's Battery and Fort Clinton to the east were part of several fortifications running approximately from Third Avenue to the Hudson River during the Revolutionary War and were used again for the War of 1812. They were manned first by British and German soldiers against the Americans during the British occupation of Manhattan from 1776 to 1783 and then by American volunteers against the British soldiers in 1814. During those times Long Island Sound and the widespread tidal marsh and meadows extending to the East River could be viewed across the Harlem Plain from this strategic site. The bluff dips into a gorge named McGown's Pass on the east edge, then rises quickly again on the far side to Fort Clinton, which was named for DeWitt Clinton, mayor of New York, 1803–1815. We will enter McGown's Pass from the water's edge farther along on this walk.

Return to the path around the water. As you pass the base of this rugged promontory, study the formation of the rock outcrop itself. Examine the vertical fissures along the jagged rock behind lamppost #0810A. These probably resulted from splitting the rock during the construction of the park. As you pass farther around the promontory, notice that the rock becomes smoother and weathered, indicating that it was left untouched during construction. This promontory and all the rock outcrops in the park have a history almost as old as the continent itself. Underlying New York City, three major rock formations can be found: Manhattan schist, Inwood marble, and Fordham gneiss. The proper names of the rock types refer to their presence in those particular areas. Manhattan schist comprises 90 percent of the rock type in Manhattan. Inwood marble, which reaches into only the north of Central Park, is the bedrock of the Harlem Plain. Fordham gneiss dips into the northeast of Manhattan from the Bronx and not into Central Park at all.

All three rock formations are metamorphic, begun aeons ago as sediments on the floor of an ancient sea that stretched from Canada to Georgia roughly along the line of the Appalachian Mountains. During the course of many millions of years the earth's molten, unstable core erupted beneath the sea, heating, compressing, and heaving up the sediments during geological events called orogenies, or mountain building. About the time of the first signs of single-celled life 450 million years ago, the Taconic orogeny heaved up other rock formations from the sea that covered the Manhattan schist and created a mountain several thousand feet high. The adamantine schist formed the core of the mountain as the mountain's weight pushed the schist deep into the earth. After many more millions of years, the mountain, as all mountains do, eroded. By the time the dinosaurs were roaming the earth, the mountain had disappeared. As the mountain was eroding, its weight decreased, allowing the schist to rise proportionately from the molten core. When the mountain was gone the schist remained at the level it is today. The promontory at the edge of the Meer, composed of Manhattan schist, is the stump of that eroded mountain.

Continue around the promontory to where the path veers off to the right at lamppost #0726 to McGown's Pass. This route, established by Native Americans, was used by travelers coming from Albany and Boston to Manhattan up until the mid-1800s. At that time, the city of Manhattan terminated at about 14th Street. The rural landscape north of it was occupied by country homes, farms, and factories. Harlem Creek and the tidal marsh surrounding it forced travelers to depart the open Harlem Plain and travel into the woods beyond the bluffs. Boston Post Road and Albany Post Road joined at the edge of the marsh before continuing south through McGown's Pass.

The path off to the right returns to Nutter's Battery. To the left the path winds up to Fort Clinton where cannon were mounted during the War of 1812. At the time of the Revolutionary War an earthen bunker connected these two bluffs. A wooden gate, which stood approximately where the paths diverge today, closed off the pass. Move straight ahead up the steps to the crest of the hill where the landscape flattens out. Across the path and beyond the lawn, a cliff rises behind the trees. A closer examination of the cliff will reveal the remnants of a stone foundation with a history older than the forts.

Travelers, then as now, preferred to arrive refreshed at their destinations and, just as we have rest stops along our interstate highways, earlier travelers had taverns or halfway houses along their routes. Five of these taverns once occupied present-day upper Central Park; the earliest one was built in 1684 to the west of McGown's Pass. The foundation—visible up ahead—began as the Dyckman Tavern in the early 1700s and was sold to the McGown family, who operated the tavern until 1845. The Sisters of Charity of Saint Vincent de Paul acquired the property in 1847, adding residences and classroom buildings. The Sisters were displaced in 1856 by the Parks commissioners and the new buildings were used as the park's administrative offices.

The Sisters of Charity returned during the Civil War, when the buildings operated as a hospital for wounded soldiers. After the war, the Sisters again relocated and the hospital became a sculpture museum; it burned down in 1881. A restaurant was built on the spot in the mid-1880s, but after it burned down, too, nothing was rebuilt on the old foundations, ending two centuries of tavern history.

Today the stone foundation remains a curiosity. The ground above it, from 105th Street to 106th Street behind the Conservatory Garden, now serves as the park's compost site where leaves and wood chips are recycled as mulch for new planting beds. The compost area is still known as The Mount, after Mount St. Vincent's.

Return to lamppost #0726 and continue on the path around the water heading east from McGown's Pass. Farther along, another set of stairs leads through the trees to the promontory where Fort Clinton sits. A planting of cardinal flower, bayberry, rushes, swamp magnolia, joe-pye weed, and pickerel weed was installed along the water's edge in 1993 to complement the connection between the looming promontory and level water. As of this writing a fence protects the dense vegetation from trampling; the success of the planting after the fence comes down will depend on how well the plants establish themselves and how respectful park users will be toward them.

Scan the water for fish that take advantage of the small, shade-protected cove near the shore. When the Meer was drained for restoration in 1990 most of the fish were seine-netted and removed to other water bodies in the park. When restoration was completed and the Meer filled again, the water was restocked with fish. In a public ceremony attended by many jubilant fishermen, thousands of largemouth bass, bull-head, catfish, and smaller fish were released. Today a catch-and-release fishing policy is enjoyed by many, including egrets and herons that seem not to observe the release policy.

The walk ends ahead where the path reconnects a few yards west from the path on which the walk began. Directly ahead, the Conservatory Garden deserves a side tour. It offers four seasons of diverting plant textures and colors, sculpture, and architecture. There are three gardens within the Conservatory Garden: the North Garden, designed after the French style; the Central, after the Italian; and the South, after the English. The North Garden hosts a spectacle of hundreds of tulips in late April and hundreds of chrysanthemums in October. These luxuriant plantings, celebrating spring and autumn, encircle the Untermeyer Fountain of the *Three Dancing Maidens* by Walter Schott, a German sculptor who died in 1938. The Central Garden, formal and expansive, boasts an ornate arbor, covered in May with the purple blossoms of Chinese wisteria, *Wisteria floribunda,* and two spectacular crab apple allees. The South Garden, a favorite lunchtime gathering place, features a memorial statue to Frances Hodgson Burnett, children's story writer and author of the legendary *The Secret Garden*. The statue is surrounded by an especially felicitous planting, including the heavily scented, spidery-looking *Nicotiana*, which is related to the tobacco plant; *Buddleia*, known as the the butterfly magnet; rose hedges; magnolias; and many other textural and colorful plantings arranged in an artfully informal manner.

Reservoir Walk

The Jacqueline Kennedy Onassis Reservoir,
Fifth Avenue and 90th Street

THIS WALK BEGINS at Engineer's Gate, on Fifth Avenue and 90th Street, and includes three ornate bridges, the second-largest tree in Central Park, some spectacular views across the half-mile wide reservoir, the first leg of Rhododendron Mile, and more.

Engineer's Gate, also known by its contemporary nickname "Runner's Gate," is the starting point of many of the New York Road Runners Club's nearly one hundred annual events. A kiosk, usually occupied by a volunteer, stands inside the gate across the road (the East Drive) and provides information about safety and various events run by the nonprofit club, which was founded in 1958. The club's headquarters, located at 9 East 89th Street (now Fred Lebow Place, in honor of the late charismatic organizer of the original New York City Marathon), welcomes the public inside for classes, publications, merchandise, and rest room facilities. Running is one of two major attractions of the reservoir's 1.5-mile cinder track. The other attraction is bird-watching. The 106-acre, 25-feet

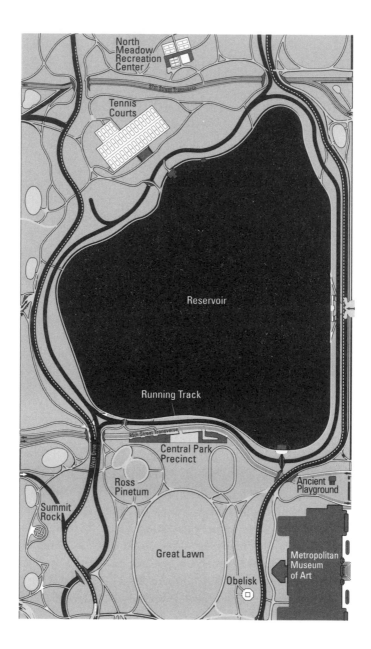

deep reservoir, the largest water body in Central Park, attracts many of the waterfowl species not observed elsewhere in the park.

Once inside the gate, the East Drive runs in a straight line for nearly half a mile north and south from 86th to 95th Street and is known as Rhododendron Mile (discussed at the end of

Rhododendron

this walk). The longest straight line in Central Park, it presented a serious design dilemma for Olmsted and Vaux, who had to contend with the unsightly eastern wall of the reservoir as well as the narrow corridor between the reservoir and Fifth Avenue. They resolved the problem by screening Fifth Avenue and the wall of the reservoir with trees and shrubs.

Across the drive from Engineer's Gate, look for an enormous 53-inch diameter English elm, *Ulmus procera,* standing sentinel on the bridle path. Although certainly large, it is not the largest tree in the park. That honor belongs to another English elm, located east of the Mall at 60th Street. (The second-largest tree in the park, a London plane, will be encountered later on this tour.) An elm this size is easily over one hundred years old and is certainly an original planting. Horticulturists of every administration have lavished attention on this elm, evidenced by the cabling work supporting the lower branches and by the frequent pruning it receives. That this elm survives at all, rooted beneath a compacted bridle path at the edge of one of the busiest thoroughfares in the city, calls for applause for those who maintain it.

On the far western side of the bridle path, the gilded bronze bust of John Purroy Mitchel rests between two urns placed on marble pilasters. Mitchel holds the honor of being New York's youngest mayor, at thirty-four, in 1914. Popular as a fusion party reformer, he fell out of favor through his association with the city's wealthy patrons and lost his bid for reelection in 1917. He died the following year in a plane crash, training for World War One.

The tour proceeds up the staircase on the right to lamppost #9002. No hard and fast rules govern use of the running track, though some protocol should be observed. The suggested direction for moving around the track is counterclockwise, and though runners do not have preference, their velocity alone earns them some leeway.

Maintenance of the track and the reservoir itself officially belongs to the Department of Environmental Protection (DEP). The DEP maintains the two gatehouses located on the north and south perimeters of the reservoir. DEP personnel also periodically remove the tree saplings growing through the riprap wall around the water, but daily maintenance of the running track and the surrounding bridle path area—the picking up of trash, repairing damage to fences, installing erosion cribbing, and filling divots in the cinder paths—falls to a zone gardener funded by the Central Park Conservancy.

The first two trees to the right of lamppost #9002 are silver lindens, *Tilia tomentosa*. This species of linden originates from China and, because of its heat and drought tolerance, is the best of the linden species for urban planting. Lindens have several other common names: among them are basswood, lime tree, and wicopy, from the Algonquin Indian name. The four species of European and Oriental lindens in the park differ from the American linden, *Tilia americana,* notably in leaf size. The leaves of the alien species range from 2 to 4 inches, whereas the American linden leaves grow from 4 to 6 inches.

Across from the lindens a yellow diamond shape is stenciled onto a black rectangle at the base of the cyclone fence.

Wild cherry

This is one of several distance markers placed around the track to help runners pace themselves. A runner's map is now available at the Road Runners Club that allows joggers to plot several courses throughout the park with distances from one-quarter mile to the six-mile circumference of the park's main drive.

As you move along to the next lamppost, notice the number of desire paths leading off the track like spokes on a wheel. Some measures have been taken to decrease use of these paths with dense plantings, such as those surrounding the Mitchel Memorial stairs, which help to deflect some of the foot traffic. The strategy here is to protect sensitive locations but allow a few of the less frequented, unofficial paths to remain, a necessary concession to park users who don't understand the damage they do.

Between the running track and the bridle path, numerous ornamental cherry trees, *Prunus spp.,* accent the reservoir's perimeter. They can be recognized by their dark scaly bark and splendid display of large showy blossoms in April and May. On the right, a few feet past lamppost #9104, a plaque embedded in a large rock reads: "These cherry trees presented to the City of New York in memory of Otto Marx: 1870–1963" (Marx was a prominent Eastsider). In mid-April, a rim of Yoshino cherry blossoms lines the east edge of the running track and then, in early May, the blossoming Kwanzan cherry trees ornament both the east and west edges of the reservoir with their starry pink splendor. These trees are particularly striking when viewed from across the water. The oldest of the flowering cherries date back to 1912, when they were presented to Central Park as gifts from Japan. Since then many of the short-lived trees have been replaced after succumbing to time and urban stress.

Not only are these cherry trees weakened by urban stress, they are also susceptible to numerous diseases and pests. Especially harmful is the tiny insect known as San Jose scale, *Aspidiotus perniciosus* (the species name comes aptly from the word *pernicious*), which feeds on the trees by literally sucking the life juices out of them. The insect arrived in California in the 1870s from China and spread quickly throughout the country, causing billions of dollars in crop damage. When the older cherry trees die, replacements are planted around the bridle path to fill the gaps opened by the demise of their elders.

Past lamppost #9202 one of several stencils on the cement base of the fence reminds bike riders that the running track is off-limits to them. This is one of the few locations in the park where biking, in-line skating, and dog-walking are not in evidence. Officially, bikes are not allowed off the main drive, though this rule is routinely ignored on most hard-surface paths. Bikers irresponsibly contribute to the severe erosion problems suffered by sensitive park landscapes and are a major cause of the eroded hillocks and trampled shrubbery.

With that in mind, it is pleasurable to be in a nearly bike-free environment surrounded only by foot traffic and the sweeping vistas of the New York skyline.

About fifty feet past lamppost #9202, another yellow stencil with a black triangle and five dots marks the 200-yard point from the stairs at the Mitchel Memorial. From here a topographical change becomes evident along Fifth Avenue. At the beginning of the tour on 90th Street the park and Fifth Avenue were at the same elevation. Heading north from 90th Street, the elevation of Fifth Avenue steadily recedes into the topographical depression that once settled into the tidal marsh of Harlem Creek, from which today's Harlem Meer was carved. The park's topography north of 90th Street, unlike the steady decline in elevation of Fifth Avenue, undulates at much the same level it did before there was a Central Park, before the streets and avenues were cut and filled to make way for the expanding needs of the growing city. The same topographical shift is mirrored, in reverse, on the West Side and explained in the 100th Street Pool Walk.

At the line of 96th Street, the track curves west. On the horizon of Fifth Avenue at 100th Street, the black monolith of Mt. Sinai Hospital appears like a blank road sign deflecting traffic around the reservoir. The Mt. Sinai building has the dubious distinction of being more visible from the upper park than any other building on the north end, though it does act as a beacon to visitors who might otherwise lose their way.

At the right edge of the bridle path beyond lamppost #9614, a large London plane tree, *Platanus acerifolium,* is believed to be the oldest tree in Central Park and, at 61 inches in diameter, the second largest. This London plane may have been planted when the reservoir was dug into the landscape, at a time that predates formal park planting in this area. At the turn of the century London planes were marketed as "super trees," with the ability to withstand all manner of abuse and disease, but time has proven otherwise. They are susceptible to a number of diseases, including the fungus disease, *Anthracnose,* a serious problem with the American sycamore, from which the London plane was hybridized with the Chinese sycamore. The London planes' resistance to this disease was once flaunted, and hundreds of thousands of London planes were distributed to urban parks throughout the world. Those problems notwithstanding, the London plane, as seen here, can mature into an admirably handsome tree when it can spread out and display its individual character.

The best waterfowl spotting, particularly during migration season and over the winter, is to be had along this northern stretch of the reservoir from the concrete base of the cyclone fence. The embankment around the reservoir provides protection from the cold north and westerly winds that cut across the open water in winter. Gulls, year-round residents of the reservoir and seemingly impervious to the cold, flock to the center of the water where they are difficult to identify without a good pair of binoculars. The three species of reservoir gulls are the ring-billed gull, the most common and most easily identified by the black ring around its bill; the herring gull, which is the largest of the gray-mantled gulls; and the great black-backed gull, our largest gull, whose slate-colored back has given it the nickname the "coffin carrier." Two occasional visitors of the gull family include the laughing gull, so named because its call resembles human laughter, and the Iceland gull, a rare, white-winged gull whose winter range occasionally includes Central Park.

Most other bird species on the reservoir are migratory—passing through or wintering over but flying north in spring. Some of the more common waterfowl to look for include canvasbacks, ruddy ducks, lesser scaups, northern shovelers, bufflehead, and gadwalls. On colder winter days these birds often frequent the north and west edges of the water, where the wind is mildest and the warming morning sun strikes first. Throughout the winter the waterfowl feed on the fish and algae and on the seeds of the many woody and herbaceous plants anchored in the rocky riprap embankment. Although the DEP removes tree saplings to prevent their roots from undermining the embankment, several herbaceous species—phragmite, mugwort, aster, several weedy knotweeds, and grasses among them—that don't threaten the embankment are left to grow, leaving their seeds to feed some of the birds. The 1982 *Central Park Wildlife Inventory* recorded bass, carp, sunfish, trout, perch, pickerel, and eels living in the reservoir.

Red-tailed hawk

In summertime, the sleek jet-black cormorant can often be seen diving beneath the reservoir and resurfacing with a fish which it gobbles down. And in winter the common loon, notorious for its eerie nocturnal, human-sounding cries, visits the park. Imagine the reaction of residents on Central Park West, hearing the cry of the loon in the dead of night. How could they not wonder if some treachery was afoot in Central Park?

At the first of the two north gatehouse buildings a stencil marks "½ mile" from 90th Street. Because the reservoir no longer serves water to the city, these two northern gatehouses are not manned. The reservoir was taken off-line after completion of a new water tunnel that brings fresh water to the city from a reservoir in Yonkers. The new water tunnel, the largest in the world at over twenty feet in diameter, crosses deep beneath the park on its way to Long Island City.

The fate of Central Park's reservoir has not been decided. It still receives water from the Croton Reservoir System, but a looming question remains: Should the flow of water into the reservoir be stopped? Without the inflow from the Croton system, evaporation would eventually reduce the reservoir's 106 water-filled acres into a gaping mud flat. Two major issues dominate the debate: If the reservoir continues to be fed by the Croton system, should the large water body be redesigned for recreational use—swimming, fishing, boating—or should the reservoir remain fenced and be redesigned as a wildlife habitat, including the addition of an island, as was done in the Harlem Meer and Turtle Pond? Today, as many constituents clamor for more active recreational facilities in Central Park, an equally loud voice calls for including space for wildlife habitat and keeping the reservoir's 106 acres fenced off. The voice of the eminent naturalist Aldo Leopold in his 1953 essay, "Wilderness," echoes from that call:

> To the laborer in the sweat of his labor, the raw stuff of his anvil is an adversary to be conquered. So was wilderness an adversary to the pioneer. But to the laborer in repose, able for a moment to cast a philosophical eye on his world, that same raw stuff is something to be loved and cherished, because it gives definition and meaning to his life. This is a plea for the preservation of some tag-ends of wildness, as museum pieces, for the edification of those who may one day wish to see, feel, or study the origins of their cultural inheritance.

In a glade across the bridle path from the gatehouse, the tennis court concession building offers refreshments and public rest rooms. The tennis courts were added to the park early this century, a political indulgence viewed by many as yet another intrusion on Olmsted and Vaux's vision. Nonetheless, the tennis courts, integral to the park today, garner thousands of dollars annually. Although that may not justify its existence aesthetically—a small meadow occupied the glade before the tennis courts were built—many worse features have been suggested for the park, including the small airport proposed after World War One and a 30,000-car underground parking lot. To play tennis a permit must be acquired at a nominal fee; inquire within for details.

Past the gatehouse at the line of 94th Street, a cast-iron bridge crosses over the bridle path connecting the running track to the tennis courts. This bridge, another of Calvert Vaux's masterworks, has the official designation of Bridge No. 28. Because not all the parks bridges received numbers, its more appealing unofficial name is Gothic Bridge, befitting the style of its bulging curves and gemlike contour of arches. Because the cast iron was not maintained over the years, weather damage slowly corroded the structure and the bridge had to be restored in the mid-1980s, using the artful foundry techniques of the nineteenth century. In the early years of the park the bridle path carried much more equestrian traffic than it does today, and the lavish bridge allowed park pedestrians to cross the bridle path without interference from horses and carriages. Equestrians still use the bridle path now, but joggers and dog walkers outnumber them.

The largest stand of turkey oaks, *Quercus cerris,* in the park begins as the running track turns south at the line of 91st Street. Turkey oaks are recognized by their dark, plated bark and small, tightly lobed leaves that resemble diminutive white oak leaves. This tree's common name refers to its origin in the

Republic of Turkey. The oaks intermingle here with a few other tree species before forming a contiguous stand along the northern edge of the 85th Street Transverse Road. Four hundred turkey oaks were counted throughout the park in 1982, making it the third most common of the fourteen oak species

Turkey oak

in the park. The pin oak and the red oak are first and second respectively. Three hundred of those four hundred turkey oaks are found around the western and southern edges of the reservoir. Turkey oaks are touted by some bird-watchers as the best tree to observe migrating warblers in spring, as the birds feed on the insects that are nurtured by the trees' thick bark and clinging dead wood.

Ornamental cherry trees and crab apples are intermingled with the turkey oaks at this point. The number of cherry trees increases on this western side of the track, forming an allee that literally buzzes with bees when the trees are displaying their springtime pink and white flowers. When the cherries are in flower, the view across the nearly half-mile wide reservoir offers a splendid spectacle of dappled blossoms.

Down the slope from lamppost #8907, two rare trees in the park bring some diversity to the limited species around the track. These medium-size atlas cedars, *Cedrus atlantica*, well rooted on the edge of a small hollow, exhibit their unique windswept form and blue-green hues. Only five atlas cedars (so named because they originate from the Atlas Mountains in Northern Africa) were counted in *The 1982 Tree Inventory*.

Two other points of interest at lamppost #8907 should be noted. An example of erosion control can be viewed here where some of the exposed cribbing boards jut out from the trampled area to the right of the lamp. Unfortunately, the cribbing is being used as steps, exacerbating the erosion problem rather than preventing it. Cribbing works as an erosion control measure only when left alone long enough to stabilize the soil. The other detail here is the apparent grafting of a young black cherry tree and a young turkey oak immediately to the left of the lamp. Black cherries often sprout up from the bases of other trees wherever their highly viable seeds find a bit of soil. Lawn mowers and string trimmers usually remove the prolific cherries before their roots get established. However, two of the places least affected by lawn mowers or string trimmers are rock outcrops and the bases of trees where the cherry seedlings often establish. This oak and cherry do not actually share the same cambium, but the coarse texture of each species' bark makes it appear as though they have.

Continue on to where the track curves left along the southern edge of the reservoir, past the "1 mile" marker stenciled on the base of the fence. The plant palette diversifies here from

Black cherry

turkey oaks and cherries to various shrubs and smaller trees. At lamppost #8639, a stand of hawthorns, recognized by their light-gray, platy bark and distinctive thorns, marks this shift to the east. The hawthorns are well placed as a landscape transition, but their vigor and longevity will be short-lived given the trampled, compacted conditions they must endure here.

At lamppost #8633 another cast-iron bridge designed by Vaux and built in 1864 spans the bridle path. Officially named Bridge No. 27, it is easier to locate by its unofficial name, Reservoir Bridge Southwest. This seventy-two-foot curved span over the bridle path also directed foot traffic over and away from the equestrians earlier in the century. Lack of maintenance caused the bridge to rust and corrode so badly that missing parts had to be redesigned during its restoration in the late 1970s. In 1989, groups of volunteers planted a ground cover of Boston ivy, scattered with daffodils, at the corners of the bridge. Much of the ivy remains to give the accent intended, especially in March and April when the daffodils flower.

Across the bridge, two paths diverge east and west. The east path parallels then connects with the 85th Street Transverse Road. The west path crosses over the transverse to the Ross Pinetum, which contains the largest grouping of evergreens—seven hundred pine trees, cedars, and spruces—in the park.

At lamppost #8627, the effectiveness of the sunken transverse roads (their design is described on the Turtle Pond Walk) can be appreciated. Traffic noise distinctly increases at this point, as vehicles pass by the gate that opens through the wall onto the 85th Street Transverse Road. Except, at this opening, the vehicular sounds are a distant, muffled background noise.

At the south gatehouse past lamppost #8522, is the Southeast Reservoir Bridge, officially known as Bridge No. 24. This third and final bridge across the bridle path was restored in 1989 by the Central Park Conservancy; the concrete deck was replaced with a wooden deck, which more befits the bridge's turn-of-the-century style. The smaller of the three reservoir bridges designed by Vaux, it has a flat rather than curved deck design. Because the bridge links the running track with the East Drive and the Metropolitan Museum of Art, it receives the most foot traffic, evidenced by the desire paths bounding off its corners, due in large part to the muddied conditions below the bridge where inadequate drainage creates an impassable quagmire at this low point of the bridle path.

The tour crosses the bridge to visit the restored sections of Rhododendron Mile, which begins on the southeast corner of the bridge and continues north to approximately 89th Street. In mid-April, a colorful display of Virginia bluebells and other springtime bulbs speckle the ground beneath the foliage of the shrubs. Then, in late May and well into June, the rhododendrons and azaleas display their spectacle of showy flowers. Rhododendron Mile was named for the plants along this stretch (actually only one-half mile, to 96th Street) in 1908 by Samuel Parsons, the gifted horticulturist who was dedicated to Central Park. Thousands of rhododendrons, a gift of Mrs. Russell Sage, a park benefactor, were planted here and came to be known as the Sage Plantation.

Samuel Parsons was a staunch supporter of Olmsted's standards and considered Central Park New York's greatest treasure. He was hired by Vaux in 1882 as Chief Horticulturist and remained at the park until 1911, when he resigned as Superintendent of Parks. Unfortunately, he resigned disgruntled over park managerial abuses, such as the addition of statuary and structures, severe funding cuts, especially in horticulture, and the tampering with the Greensward Plan, Olmsted and Vaux's original design, by dividing the pastoral landscape into special interest features.

Over the years the Parsons rhododendrons have succumbed to neglect. Sporadic attempts have been made to return this stretch of the park to its turn-of-the-century splendor, but because rhododendrons are fussy about their habitat, that was never an easy task. Rhododendrons are woodland and wetland species of the heath family, adaptable to formal landscapes only if properly maintained. In urban parks, maintenance in the long term is never guaranteed. A 1991 restoration of the 86th Street entrance off Fifth Avenue included a portion of Rhododendron Mile from 86th to 89th Street. A stroll along that portion of East Drive will be most rewarding from late May through June when the rhododendrons, azaleas, and various wildflowers along the three-block section are in full blossom. A zone gardener, funded by one of Fifth Avenue's park-loving philanthropists, now maintains the area indefinitely. Continuation of the Rhododendron Mile restoration awaits other donors.

The walk ends here, with words from William K. Stevens, author of *Miracle Under the Oaks: The Revival of Nature in America,* a constructive account of the rebuilding of ecosystems by uniting such disciplines as ecology, biology, botany, ornithology, natural history, sociology, volunteerism, and whatever else it takes to restore our precious wildlands, of which Central Park may be considered at least a fragment:

> The new restorationists view their enterprise as a healing art. Some see themselves as physicians whose patients are ecosystems. Just as a doctor intervenes to treat a patient injured in an automobile accident so that healing can proceed, so restorationists intervene to repair the damage caused by other humans so that the natural evolutionary processes that generate biodiversity can resume. . . . The restorationists are finding that putting nature back together is a daunting and humbling business.

Turtle Pond Walk

Turtle Pond,
81st Street and Central Park West

TO BEGIN THE walking tour, enter the park at 81st Street and Central Park West and follow the path across West Drive to the Delacorte Theater, where you will see statues honoring two of Shakespeare's plays.

This walk includes the Shakespeare Garden, the Delacorte Theater, Belvedere Castle, a memorial to a Polish king, and a pond that is home to turtles, dragonflies, and a number of visiting and permanent waterfowl, along with an interesting array of trees, shrubs, and wildflowers. Also included on this walk is a brief history of the Great Lawn, which was once a major drinking-water reservoir for New York City and of which Turtle Pond is a remnant.

The Delacorte Theater, built in 1960, hosts the Shakespeare-in-the-Park Festival, which features two of Shakespeare's plays each summer. The festival was founded and directed by the late Joseph Papp, who also founded the non-profit Public Theater. Papp's productions remained true to Shakespeare's intent by staging the plays as entertainment for

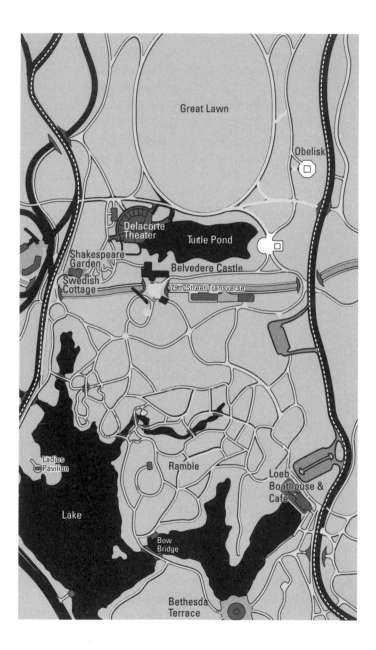

the general public. Stars such as Kevin Klein, Denzel Washington, Tracy Ullman, Morgan Freeman, Patrick Stewart, and the late Raul Julia have all entertained audiences who come to see the plays free of charge, first come, first served.

The two statues, *The Tempest* and *Romeo and Juliet,* were sculpted by Milton Hebald in 1966 and 1977, respectively, and were contributed to the park by George Delacorte, a philanthropist and theater lover, who also paid half the cost for construction of the theater. *The Tempest* statue was dedicated to Joseph Papp.

Before beginning the main tour, let's take a brief bird-watching side tour by taking the path north from the statues to lamppost #8145 positioned in front of a sizable pin oak. The nearby pin oak is part of a two-acre stand of oaks and black locusts, stretching from this point north to the Ross Pinetum, where four acres are the habitat to seven hundred pine, including more than fifteen species.

Within the stand of oak and locust the breadth of the tree canopy makes the area especially attractive to a rich variety of birds. The locusts offer thick bark and tenacious dead limbs, a perfect habitat for insects and insect-eating birds such as woodpeckers and warblers. While the warblers tap lightly with their beaks at the loose bark, the woodpeckers hunt for insects by chiseling openings into the tree trunk; the openings provide nesting sites for other species. The 1982 *Central Park Wildlife Inventory* compiled by John Hecklau lists eleven cavity-nesting birds known to breed in Central Park, including the tufted titmouse, the black-capped chickadee, the white-breasted nuthatch, the common flicker, and the very aggressive European starling, which often displaces other birds from the cavities. Nesting birds can be observed in these trees from spring through midsummer. Also in the inventory of 1982, the author notes that forty-two species of birds have been recorded nesting in the park since the 1880s and that about twenty species still nest regularly. With a little patience and observation many of the nest builders can be detected by watching for birds with construction materials in their beaks, such as strands of grass, paper, or plastic, and then following them to their destination. Later in spring and summer, be alert to those same birds flying to their nests with food, mostly worms or insects, for their chicks.

Willow oak

Return to the statues, where we will begin the Turtle Pond Walk. Head east past the three willow oaks, *Quercus phellos,* on the right—two inside the pipe rail and a smaller one outside. These trees are recognized by their narrow, long (three to five inches) leaves with a bristle tip at the end and by their dark, shallow-grooved bark. Willow oaks are native to the southern mixed hardwood forests that range from Maryland through Louisiana, but they fare well in Central Park and other urban parks because they resist pollution and adapt well to a variety of soil conditions. Because of their ability to survive the city's tough demands, willow oaks are often used as street trees. Here the willow oaks add a soft vertical touch to the broad, curved structure of the Delacorte Theater.

Beyond the oaks and a line of hawthorns along the fence, a view over the water reveals Turtle Pond and Belvedere Castle.

Seen from this vantage point, the castle emerges from the craggy outcrop like a weighty fortress surrounded by a broad moat, but it didn't always appear this way. Before construction of Central Park began in 1857, the Great Lawn was the old receiving reservoir in the Croton Aqueduct system, supplying water to New York City until 1929. Turtle Pond is a remnant of that reservoir, which was drained after the new reservoir (a few blocks north of here and visited on the Reservoir Walk) began serving water to the city.

After a shantytown developed in the old reservoir's pit during the Depression, Robert Moses, Parks Commissioner from 1934 until 1960, created the Great Lawn by filling in the drained reservoir and leaving Turtle Pond to serve as a catch basin for storm water drainage. Moses named the water body Belvedere Lake, and it remained so until the 1980s when Parks Commissioner Henry Stern renamed it Turtle Pond, in honor of the numerous turtles that inhabit the water.

Commissioner Moses landscaped the thirty-acre Great Lawn with flagstone walkways, trees, shrubs, and turf, which included a perimeter of flowering cherry trees, many still flowering from late March through April. By 1995, after sixty years of poor drainage, erosion, and trampling from ball playing and other activities, the Parks Department and the Central Park Conservancy were prompted to relandscape the Great Lawn and Turtle Pond. As of this writing the project is transforming the landscape by upgrading recreational facilities and providing educational space for programs run out of the Henry Luce Learning Center located inside Belvedere Castle.

The restoration of the Great Lawn and Turtle Pond also includes developing the pond for wildlife habitat by installing an island and improving the pond's edges to foster a diversity of aquatic life, from insects to reptiles to birds. The design and use of the restored Turtle Pond was in large part inspired by the current movement to educate the city's youth to the ways of science and nature by offering Central Park as a nature observatory. In 1860, when the park was under construction, 80 percent of the nation's population resided in rural areas; by 1990 that statistic reversed and today 75 percent of the nation's population resides in urban areas. Activities that were once familiar to children at the turn of the century, such as catching frogs, marveling at nesting birds in one's own back-yard, turning over rocks in a stream to search for crayfish, gamboling through fields, picking fresh fruit from a tree, or just experiencing the soft tones of a woodland or waterway, are no longer commonplace. As early as 1949, the great natu-ralist Aldo Leopold, in his essay "Natural History," lamented our separation from nature, especially as it was taught in the classroom:

> The science of relationships is called ecology, but what we call it matters nothing. The question is, does the educated citizen know he is only a cog in the eco-logical mechanism? That if he will work with that mechanism his mental wealth and his material wealth can expand indefinitely? But that if he refuses to work with it, it will ultimately grind him to dust? If educa-tion does not teach us these things, then what is edu-cation for?

Since Leopold's time the importance of ecology and an understanding of the environment has been ingrained into all of our systems, from education and economics to politics and even religion, as the earth itself has again attained a sacred sta-tus. In 1992, the Dana Discovery Center began administering environmental education programs to the city's public and private schools. That commitment continued in 1996 with the inclusion of the Henry Luce Learning Center at Belvedere Castle.

Where the paths diverge ahead, continue along to the right to the statue of the Polish king Jagiello, poised boldly on his agitated horse, his swords raised and crossed, as he lords over the pond high on his pedestal. King Jagiello, the Grand Duke of Lithuania, united his country with Poland when he married the Polish queen. He is immortalized here in the Battle of Grunwald against the Teutons in 1410. To express the solidarity of his country against the Germans, the Polish sculptor Stanislaw Ostrowski entered this statue in the 1939 World's Fair at approximately the time of the German invasion of Poland. After the war the Polish government bestowed the work on New York City.

On Saturdays and Sundays throughout the summer months, traditional folk dancing can be enjoyed on the oval tarmac between the King and Turtle Pond. Folk music from Eastern Europe, South America, Ireland, and the United States fills the air while dancers, some in traditional garb, hop and kick and shuffle rhythmically before the King. Many of the participants are regular attendees of this mini–folk festival, dancing in circles before a Polish King in the center of a huge urban park in the hub of a vast city. The sense that they convey is one of a harmonious gathering in a small village where familiarity, neighborliness, and friendship fill the air no less than the lively music. All are welcomed to the dance and the experience is a unique one, even in a city that offers as much diversity as New York.

Between the water's edge and the tarmac, a grooved rock outcrop slants into the water, gouged out by the Wisconsin glacier ten to fifteen thousand years ago. (The Wisconsin ice is discussed at length in the 59th Street Pond Walk.) The glacier-carved rock offers a relaxed setting in which to pause and consider the pond's wildlife. Throughout the year, Turtle Pond is a rewarding place to watch the cycles of aquatic life. Known to some as the Dragonfly Preserve, the pond bustles with dragonfly activity, and the entire life cycle of the dragonfly can be observed here. Over five thousand species of dragonflies inhabit the ponds and lakes around the world with four hundred of those species found in North America.

Dragonflies have voracious appetites and consume huge quantities of mosquitoes and flies. H. T. Fernald, in his *Applied Entomology* of 1926, reports of attempts to tame dragonflies and keep them in houses to feed on flies and "one specimen having been known to consume forty houseflies in less than two hours." In addition to their appetites, dragonflies are extremely territorial. Males stake out territory over the pond then ferociously defend it against other males.

After mating, the female dragonfly finds a suitable place along the water's edge to deposit her eggs. The emerging nymphs, less than an inch in length, prowl around the submerged vegetation for insects and the occasional small fish to satisfy their ravenous appetites. The following season the nymphs emerge from the water as adults.

The wary turtles, for which Turtle Pond is named, are less frequently seen than the dragonflies because they disappear into the water when approached. Of the seven turtle species recorded throughout the five boroughs of New York City, three are common in Central Park and all are aquatic turtles. They are: snapping turtle, *Chelydra serpintina;* red-eared slider, *Pseudemys scripta elegans;* and eastern painted turtle, *Chrysemys picta.* Land turtles, easily captured by curious youngsters, do not survive in urban parks.

Snapping turtles are the most successful breeders of the three common species and they exist in several of Central Park's water bodies. Red-eared sliders, found in the wild farther south in the coastal states, are commonly sold in pet stores and many are released in the park when they outgrow their terrariums. They adapt well to the park's warm waters and hibernate in winter. The young sliders feed on snails, tadpoles, and insects, while the adults are mostly vegetarian. Painted turtles are the least frequently observed of the park's three common species. They feed on frogs, aquatic invertebrates, and the abundant fish in the waters. John Hecklau, in *Wildlife Inventory of Central Park,* recorded eight species of fish in Turtle Pond, including largemouth bass, yellow perch, brown bullhead, bluegill, pumpkinseed, golden shiner, and goldfish.

Return to the path. Southeast of the Polish King a stand of hawthorns, *Cratageus spp.,* spreads out and covers the hillock that descends to the East Drive. The hawthorns were prominently placed in this location so that park users have the sense of passing by a thicket or old field. In their natural environment the thirty-five species of native hawthorns grow in several forest types, including Central Park's oak-hickory type. Hawthorns are found commonly as pioneer species encroaching into thickets and old fields.

Hawthorn

The hawthorn's fruit is considered by ecologists to be a low-quality wildlife food because it contains only small amounts of lipids (fat) that are necessary to produce sustained energy. High-lipid foods, which provide twice the energy by weight as carbohydrates (sugar), are especially important to the migrating birds that require enduring energy over long flights. Hawthorns typically contain 1 to 2 percent lipids, while other vegetation in the park—dogwoods, spicebush, and Virginia creeper among them—have lipid contents of 20 to 30 percent. Migrating birds quickly consume the high-lipid fruits in autumn, leaving the low-lipid fruits, such as hawthorn, roses, mountain ash, red cedar, and poison ivy untouched. Only after the choice fruits have been eaten are the abundant fruits of the hawthorns and others consumed in winter by grateful resident bird populations.

The path diverges after King Jagiello at lamppost #F-05. We'll take the path to the right, keeping the water on the right. But first examine the large-diameter tree on the north corner of the paths. This is the thorny honey locust, *Gleditsia triacanthos,* recognized by both its dark brown, nearly black, and somewhat flaky bark and its formidable thorns, four to eight inches long, covering most of the tree from six feet above ground up to the crown. The thornless variety of honey locust, *G. triacanthos inermis,* is discussed on the 59th Street Pond Walk.

Three hundred honey locusts were recorded in the *1982 Tree Inventory,* their numbers separated evenly between thorny and thornless. Much of the honey locust provides useful resources and occupies a utilitarian niche in our history. The sixteen-inch twisted fruit pods contain nutritious seeds that were once crushed and used for cattle feed; the pods also contain a sugary

Honey locust

pulp that can be scooped and eaten or fermented into a beer, as early American settlers did. Native Americans prepared a gargle for sore throats from the bark, and hunters and frontiersmen used the thorns for spearpoints and pins. Today the dense wood, as durable as the black locust, is still used for furniture, fences, and railroad ties. Its value as a wildlife food extends to deer, rabbits, squirrels, bobwhite, and many others.

Moving along toward the next intersection of paths we ascend well above Turtle Pond. The straight, level path along this south terminus of the pond was once the southern wall of the old Croton Reservoir, which will become more evident as you walk toward Belvedere Castle. The gentle, grassy slope leading down to the water was the riprap wall of the old reservoir. From here one can imagine the old reservoir as it was: a rippling expanse of water only a few feet from the path, opened out and spreading northward along the perimeter of what is now the Great Lawn.

Today a walk along this path offers a diverse allee of trees and shrubs. On the left where the paths merge, look for a statuesque, spidery ironwood, *Carpinus betulus,* recognized by its sinewy gray bark and nodding and soaring branches. The next tree on the left and the tree across the path from it are river birches, *Betula nigra,* recognized by the dark, plated, tough reddish bark on the trunk which is often papery and peeling on younger branches. One of the tallest of our fourteen native birches, the river birch often reaches heights of ninety feet. River birches thrive at this location, which suits their natural requirements for a bottomland near water.

Red oaks, pin oaks, and younger ironwoods also line this path, together with a variety of other native shrubs such as pepperbush, dogwood, and the largest highbush blueberry in the park, located between the path and the water.

At lamppost #7932 a stand of shrubby dogwood, *Cornus* sp., forms a thicket that spreads out and down to the water.

River birch

Within this stand, a fragile habitat has developed. In autumn, leaf litter accumulates among its shrubby stems. As it does, numerous micro and macroscopic wildlife ranging from fungus to worms spread through its layers to decompose and recycle the nutrients in the leaves. This complex, fragile microsystem represents an environment commonly found in stable, healthy ecosystems, but scarcely in urban parks because of excessive disturbance. The decomposed leaf litter not only provides organic nutrients to the roots of the shrub, it also helps retain moisture during droughts and provide food for migrating birds. With that in mind, take care not to disturb these fragile habitats when encountered anywhere in the park.

At the next lamppost ahead on the left, across from the water fountain, take the stairs down to the 79th Street Transverse Road. Looking west from the bottom of the stairs, a tun-

Dogwood

nel runs through the rock outcrop. *The 1861 Annual Report of The Central Park,* compiled by the park's Board of Commissioners, reports men working day and night here blasting through the rock with dynamite and cannonballs. In the autumn of 1861, the 146-foot-long, 17-foot-10-inch-high, 40-foot-wide tunnel was complete. The traffic sounds heard here along the transverse road help us appreciate the genius of its design, which diverts traffic away from the tranquil park.

Three other sunken transverse roads, located at 66th Street, 86th Street, and 96th Street, also carry traffic east and west through the park. The transverse roads effectively eliminate traffic volume and noise in the park while providing access across town. They were originally designed for horses and carriages, but since 1899, when the first permit for an automobile to enter Central Park was issued, we became even more fortunate to have them. The first automobile permit carried the admonition that the vehicle must slow down to three miles per hour when encountering horses.

Before returning to the tour path, turn your attention to the top edge of the wall across the road and the two large red oaks that loom precipitously. Note that the roots supporting these trees grow south of the wall, while the trees, weighing several tons, lean to the north. This exerts tremendous tension on the slender threads of roots and is a testament to the strength and stability of the trees' root systems.

Our knowledge of roots has improved in the latter half of this century, and today we have a much better understanding of their symbiosis with the earth. Roots, by way of their high tensile strength, anchor plants to the ground with a core of xylem, a woody substance with thick inner cell walls, and an outer layer of softer, absorbent cells. The combination of the two creates an elasticity, like nylon, that allows the roots to stretch when high winds push at the tree or ungainly angles of growth cause it to defy gravity. The quantity of roots in a single tree also contributes to its stability. Belying conventional beliefs that the roots mirror the canopy of the tree, we now know that the feeder roots of most trees extend beyond the canopy by three or four times the canopy's spread. The total length of a mature tree's roots can be measured in hundreds of miles. Add a taproot to that, as these oaks have, and all fears of toppling should be assuaged.

Continue the tour up the stairs and stop at the castle's low wall where a commanding view stretches out over Turtle Pond and the Great Lawn toward Fifth Avenue. The austere rock outcrop below, known as Vista Rock, continues from below the wall at this spot west to Shakespeare Garden. Vista Rock presented severe design challenges for Olmsted and Vaux, who debated with the commissioners for ten years over what to do with this feature. Clarence Cook, in his 1869 *A Guide to Central Park,* wrote that Belvedere rock "has been a constant source of anxiety to the commissioners, a sort of elephant on their hands that they did not know very well how to dispose of." They settled on enlarging the elephant by building a castle on top of it. Built in the Norman-Gothic style, construction of the castle began in 1867 and cost $450,000, a considerable sum in nineteenth-century dollars. A second tower was planned for the northern wall, but a $50,000 price tag kept it from being built. After completion of the castle, the commissioners were pleased and wrote in the 1871 annual report that it is "one of the strongest and most intrinsically thorough buildings in its construction upon the Central Park."

On the south side of the castle the path veers left and right. The walk continues on the path to the right, over the three stone steps hewn from the rock leading to the castle's esplanade. The other two paths, heading south and away from the castle, veer around an area enclosed by a cyclone fence topped with razor wire. Inside the fence the city weather bureau maintains instruments that read atmospheric conditions. Data is sent daily to

Rockefeller Center, where it is distributed to newspapers, radio, and television. The bureau first tracked weather from Central Park in the 1870s with instruments—many designed by Daniel Draper, the park's first weatherman—kept in the Arsenal (64th Street off 5th Avenue), but Draper complained of the cramped, poorly lit, dusty conditions there. The observatory was then moved to the castle, where it has been ever since. Inside the castle other instruments read information gathered by the weather vane atop the tower.

From the esplanade another commanding view of the park opens out to the north and west. From the north edge of Vista Rock you can enjoy a backdoor view of Delacorte Theater. The sheer rock also attracts adventurous rock climbers who are quickly discouraged by the Park's Enforcement Patrol (PEP) and the Park Rangers.

Inside the castle, the Henry Luce Learning Center offers environmental and historical information on the natural history of Central Park. Many school groups and tourists have learned the skill of observing nature by using the Learning Center's numerous displays to examine the park's diverse and fragile array of plants and animals. It is hoped that understanding the park's delicate ecosystems will foster better park stewardship. When this generation learns the value of the park it will pass that value on to the next generation. Again, in the words of Aldo Leopold, who attempted to create a unified environmental policy decades before the environmental movement:

> Ecology is now teaching us to search in animal populations for analogies to our own problems. By learning how some small part of the biota ticks, we can guess how the whole mechanism ticks. The ability to perceive these deeper meanings, and to appraise them critically, is the woodcraft of the future.

A stairwell exits the esplanade to the west and leads through a small formal lawn with rustic benches and a wooden rail fence entwined with rose bushes. Linger here in June for a striking display of blossoms and an olfactory indulgence of rosy fragrance. The path breaks off left and right on the other side of the lawn, where the tour follows the left flagstone path that meanders into the Shakespeare Garden.

The Shakespeare Garden, along with the Conservatory Garden at 5th Avenue and 105th Street, are the only two formal gardens in the park. In the nineteenth century, the area of the Shakespeare Garden, a continuation of Vista Rock's west slope, was covered with patches of forsythia, bladdernut, columbine, and poplars. In 1916, for the 300th anniversary of Shakespeare's death, the Shakespeare Society turned the location into a commemorative garden; however, after several horticulturally apathetic administrations, the garden lost its formality to weeds and vandals. In the 1980s, the garden was restored by the Central Park Conservancy and is now maintained by a zone gardener.

Although Shakespeare wove the names of nearly two hundred trees, shrubs, wildflowers, and herbs into his plays and poetry, only about half of those enliven this garden. A few of the herbs and flowers have plaques next to them with appropriate quotes from the Bard's work. The courteous and botanically savvy zone gardener will usually identify plants for visitors, if she's not too busy weeding, watering, planting, and generally tending to the demanding needs of the garden.

In the winter of 1994–95, a saw-whet owl, *Aegolius acadicus,* a yearly migrant and the smallest bird of prey in this region at eight inches long, came to the garden for the winter. Curious about its feeding habits, some dedicated birdwatchers took it upon themselves to observe the owl through the night. Saw-whets roost in low evergreen shrubs, of which the Shakespeare Garden has many. These remarkably tame and tiny raptors allow close scrutiny, as long as they're not disturbed. The bird-watchers had hoped to catch a glimpse of the owl's nocturnal activities during some very cold evenings, and they were not disappointed. The owl's diet in the wild consists of insects and mice. But insects are dormant in winter and, according to the 1982 wildlife inventory, only the indoor house mouse, *Mus musculus,* lived in the park and would not be available to the owl. But the bird-watchers and other naturalists were pleasantly surprised after the little owl dropped out of its roost, flew off through the garden, and quickly pounced on a white-footed mouse, *Peromyscus leucopus.* Up until that time white-footed mice had not been recorded in the park.

We leave the Shakespeare Garden by following the winding flagstone path down to the two rustic benches that flank a large black mulberry, *Morus nigra,* on the left of the stairs. The mulberry reportedly originates from a cutting taken from a tree on Shakespeare's front yard at Stratford-on-Avon, his birth and burial place.

At the bottom of the stairs the path divides right and left around the Swedish Cottage. The tour will follow the path to the right, but first examine the large tree on the left across the path from the cottage. This hybrid oak, Lea's oak, *Quercus imbricaria X leana,* is a cross between the black oak, *Q.*

Mulberry

velutina, and the shingle oak, *Q. imbricaria.* The Lea's oak's noticeably broader, oblong leaves with only slight lobes easily distinguish it from other oaks in the park. Lea's oaks inhabit rich woods and marshy bottomlands from New Jersey south to Tennessee and Arkansas, and this vigorous specimen may owe its health to the landscape designer who wisely placed it at this location, where it benefits from the natural drainage that settles into this low area. The swampy south branch of the Sawkill River once meandered east along this site from Columbus Avenue before the builders of the park drained it. Construction of the park left only the Lake as its remnant. But the subsurface drainage remains much the same, and this water-loving tree benefits from the ancient basin that was created here by the Wisconsin glacier. When properly exploited, the natural features of a landscape work well with landscape design.

The Swedish Cottage (also known as the Marionette Theater) was constructed in Sweden for the 1876 Centennial Exposition in Philadelphia and placed here after the exposition ended. Puppet shows are performed in the cottage year-round. The puppets, crafted by the puppeteers and designers who operate the theater, treat children to such classic stories as "Rumplestiltskin" and "Goldilocks and the Three Bears." In the late 1980s and early 1990s, when the budget ax was wielded over the Parks Department, slashing maintenance and programs, the theater program at the cottage was spared, a testament to the remnants of humanity in the city's bureaucracy.

Follow the edge of the garden to the right along the rustic cedar fence, where a floral fanfare decorates the open space behind it. Beginning in mid-April and lasting for about two weeks, a stunning display of Virginia bluebells, *Mertensia virginica,* line the fence and spread into the areas beyond with nodding blue and pink bell-like flowers and lush, succulent, greenish purple foliage. By June the fences are accentuated with a diversity of roses and many other attractive and fragrant blossoms. Walking along this path at any time of year is a visual treat.

The path diverges in three directions ahead at the Delacorte Theater, where the Turtle Pond Walk ends.

West Lake Walk

Mid-Park at 73rd Street

THE WALK BEGINS at Bow Bridge by entering the park at 72nd Street from either Fifth Avenue or Central Park West. Bow Bridge, located mid-park between 73rd and 74th Streets, connects the Ramble to Cherry Hill and Bethesda Terrace. Along the walk we will cross three more bridges, examine the Ladies Pavilion, visit three rustic shelters, circle Cherry Hill, investigate a sealed-off cave, and examine a number of trees and shrubs.

Before beginning the walk take a moment to consider a brief history of the Ramble, believed by many to be the heart of Central Park. The innovative Frederick Law Olmsted and Calvert Vaux took advantage of the existing terrain—the natural, swampy depressions and looming rock outcrops—to create the Lake and the Ramble, which they considered the American garden. Olmsted writes:

> There can be no better place than the Ramble for the perfect realization of the wild garden and I want to stock it that way as fully and rapidly as possible. . . .

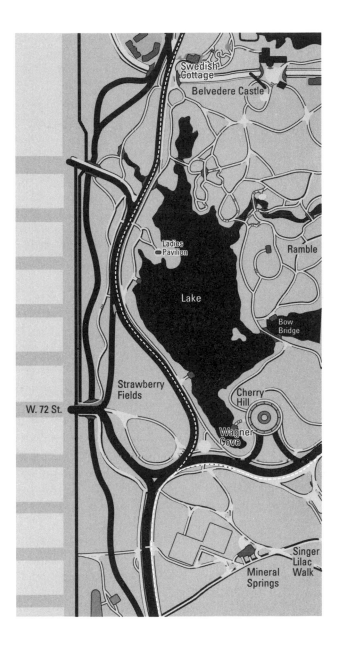

It is well sheltered, and large masses of rock occur at intervals. The soil is moist, and altogether remarkably well adapted to what is called in Europe an American garden—that is, a ground for the special cultivation of hardy plants of the natural order *Ericacae,* consisting of rhododendrons, andromedas, azaleas, kalmias, rhodoras, etc. The present growth, consisting of sweet gum, spice-bush, tulip tree, sassafras, red maple, black oak, azalea, andromeda, etc., is exceedingly intricate and interesting.

The pre-Ramble landscape was cleared of stone and "various indifferent plants" and swampy places were filled in. A lengthy stream was then created to define this wild American garden. Hundreds of trees, shrubs, and wildflowers were also planted, though not all native—a complete list of the diverse species would fill nearly ten pages, with individual plants numbering in the thousands. A partial list of native plants includes hemlock, black alder, mountain laurel, various rhododendrons, spirea, sumac, American chestnut, blueberries, several American roses, fox grape, Solomon's seal, sweet spire, tulip trees, hazelnut, yellow root, pines, and Carolina allspice.

For a little international seasoning, the plant list also included Spanish chestnut, Spanish oak, English yew, Oriental spruce, Austrian pine, European bladdernut, French rose, European larch, daffodils, and tulips and, what was later to become Central Park's scourge weed, Japanese knotweed, which at this writing continues to occupy and dominate large patches of land in the Ramble.

Olmsted's wild American garden was quickly trampled by the turn of the century, and by the 1950s, only the skeleton of the garden could be recognized. The lush composition of flora designed for "making the visitor feel as if he had got far away from the town" was slowly yielding to the footsteps of time and lack of maintenance. This, the most undulating area in the park, slowly eroded as plants and their root systems lost their grip on the soil of the Ramble's steep slopes and hillocks. Overuse and mostly unwitting abuse of the landscape by city dwellers anxious for respite from the city denuded the soil, the one element a garden cannot do without.

A $200,000 restoration project in the 1950s breathed life back into the Ramble. The addition of new topsoil and fresh plantings were welcomed by many park users, including members of the environmentally conscious Linnaean Society, who invested much time to defending the wildness of the Ramble against its errant users. The new plantings followed the intention though not the diversity of Olmsted, by incorporating many of the plants listed in his writings. Unfortunately, changing the landscape did not change the habits of its visitors. Within a decade the garden was once again spoiled and again a public outcry could be heard to restore the Ramble.

In 1979, M. M. Graff, a horticulturist as well as a staunch defender of the Olmstedian vision of Central Park, wrote a seventy-three page guideline for restoration of the Ramble. In it she cites her choices of dozens of mostly native and some carefully chosen non-native flora for the Ramble, as well as the best placement for each. The suggestions were never implemented, however, because restoration attempts ground to a halt in the early 1980s owing to an unpopular attempt by the Central Park Administrator's office to relandscape the Ramble in a way that appeared to many constituents more of a clear-cutting than a restoration.

The Ramble became a social and political front line. Flanks were sharply drawn: park management on one side; park users on the other. For a decade, no restoration was attempted in the Ramble and, season after season, as the landscape continued to be trampled, it began to look like a battlefield. Finally, in 1990, for the sake of Central Park's wild heart, the opposing sides of the debacle reconciled. The conference table was their peace table, and the unified combatants became the Central Park Woodlands Advisory Board. Since then, and very slowly, an incremental restoration has begun. One small, seriously degraded site was chosen for restoration, which will be visited on this walk. That site raised the hopes of all respectful Ramble users that each season other sites of the ravaged landscape would be selected for low-impact, incremental restoration. The partnership between the park's management and the Ramble's constituents is off to an effective start, with this caution from M. M. Graff:

> Today the Ramble bears little resemblance to Olmsted's intended forests and glades featuring locally native plant materials . . . it is always necessary to keep in mind present-day limitations imposed by overuse, soil compaction, air pollution, lack of competent horticultural care and breakdown of public discipline.

The walk begins from the Ramble side of Bow Bridge (a more detailed account of Bow Bridge is found in the East Lake Walk). Follow the path straight ahead, keeping the water on your left, and stop at the path that veers up the slope at lamppost #7413. Between the path and the undulat-

Sassafras

ing rock outcrop to the right, look for a welcoming stand of sassafras, *Sassafras albidum,* recognized by the three different shapes of the leaves on the same tree: a smooth, egg-shaped leaf, a mitten-shaped leaf (cloven-foot, symbol of the devil, was the nineteenth-century description), and a three-lobed leaf. In winter, when there are no leaves, look for the green buds. The sycamore maple, an invasive European tree, is the only other tree in Central Park with prominent green buds and is only sporadically represented in the Ramble.

Sassafras indicates that the Ramble is a true woodland, because it is a short-lived successional tree species that forms dense stands from root growths in old fields and emerging woods. Sassafras, like the red cedar and birch, prepares the way for the forest's climax trees, such as oaks and hickories, by shading out grasses and preparing the soil for those trees, which eventually become dominant in the canopy.

Sassafras was not known in pre-Columbian Europe, but once its properties were proven, it quickly gained a reputation among European herbalists. Ferdinand C. Lane reports in *The Story of Trees* that some authorities stated that "the powdered sassafras in twelve hours cured one of our company who had taken a great surfeit by eating the bellies of dog fish, a very delicious meate [*sic*]." Another observed that "the roots of sassafras hath power to comfort the liver—to comfort the weake and feeble stomacke—stay vomiting and make sweet a stinking breath."

Sassafras is ordinarily cleared from wild landscapes to make way for parkscapes because it forms solid stands and interferes with ornamental trees and shrubs. However, recent efforts to restore landscapes to native ecologies has turned native plant propagation into an industry. Pioneer nurserymen now cater to the sensitivities of native ecological restoration by growing and selling many native plant species that were once considered weeds, sassafras among them. The new landscape philosophy is based on a more natural display of native species in suitable environments. The parks of the future may in some ways be compared to zoos, with the subjects not animals but remnant forests—a collection of plant species, some endangered in the wild, storing seed banks for the future.

On the northeast corner of the path at lamppost #7413, a stand of Japanese viburnum, *Viburnum sieboldii,* reminds us that we are still in Central Park and not a rural woodlands. Although not a native to our forests, these sizable imported viburnum have showy flowers in late May and red twigs and berries throughout the summer that provide nesting opportunity and food for local wildlife. Japanese viburnum are used to accent paths and slopes, as seen here, and to soften rigid stairs, small buildings, and paths in other areas of the park.

Sour gum

Farther ahead, across from lamppost #7523, examine a mature sour gum, *Nyssa sylvatica.* This specimen has a double trunk that splits off again to form a third trunk. Recognize it also by the conspicuous, deeply grooved bark with a checkered pattern, and by the leathery, elliptic, almost rounded leaves with a short, abrupt tip. Sour gum is well suited to this site, bordering the water as it would in its natural environment. This tree is healthy despite the trampling around its surface roots because its feeder roots, far below the surface, sustain the tree above ground. The whimsical botanical name, *Nyssa sylvatica,* refers to both the nymph, Nyssa, and to the relationship with wooded (sylvan) environments; a fanciful translation might be "the woodland tree of the water nymphs." Sour gums' autumn foliage colors the sky with crimson splendor and a sour gum on the edge of a glade in the north Ramble is one of the most photographed autumnal trees in Central Park. Its berries, bitter to human taste, ripen from September into November at the peak of bird migration and provide sustenance to over thirty species of birds. The sour gum has also long been known for its utility. Its light-colored, tough lumber provides furniture, boxes, chopping bowls, gun stocks, and rollers in glass factories.

Between lamppost #7523 and the next stop on the walk at lamppost #7525, test your identification skills by locating on the right a large sweet gum, *Liquidambar styraciflua,* with star-shaped leaves, deep gray bark, and corky, ridged branches, emerging from the Japanese viburnum. Also on the right, locate an admirable black cherry, *Prunus serotina,* with broad girth, strikingly dark bark, and bold stature anchoring the far end of the same stand of viburnum. Beyond those the large, wavy-toothed leaves of common witch hazel, *Hamamelis virginiana,* with spidery yellow blossoms in midautumn, overhang the benches. On the left of the path a willow oak,

Witch hazel

Quercus phellos, stands beside an American sycamore. And on the shore of the Lake, a dense stand of arrowwood viburnum, *Viburnum dentatum,* arches into the Lake.

At lamppost #7525 a path with stairs branches off to the right. For a side tour to Azalea Pond follow the steps up from the lamppost and at the top bear left. At the intersection of paths take the path to the left with the small stream on your right. To avoid getting lost, simply keep the water on your right as you follow the loop of the path. Follow that path to the three small steps and turn right to cross the small rustic bridge formerly known as Shadow Bridge (No. 22), which crosses the brook known as the Gill, an old English word for brook. On the other side of the bridge the path arcs to the left then right to a second rustic bridge.

The larger body of water to the left of this bridge is Azalea Pond, named for the group of azaleas at the water's southern edge that have stood sentry here since the turn of the century. M. M. Graff had no kind words for these azaleas:

> Across from the cork trees, at the water's edge, is an unnatural straight line of azaleas, the garish *carmine Hinode-giri,* an offense to the eye in almost any garden setting and a shrieking dissonance in this quiet spot.

Garish or not, an unpublished report compiled by Central Park's informally organized bird-watchers in 1979 notes that these same azaleas "offer a magnificent spectacle in May" and that "ruby-throated hummingbirds, attracted to the blossoms, may be seen regularly sipping nectar." And "in winter, the tiny saw-whet owl uses the azalea bushes as a roost." The azaleas are much weakened since those observations were made, but it is hoped that improved maintenance in the Ramble will save these exotic shrubs.

Azalea Pond is arguably the premier bird-watching spot in Central Park, the virtual heart of the Ramble. On any given morning dozens of bird-watchers from around the world will drift through this area, heads bent back hoping for a glimpse at a rare warbler or welcoming the first migrants in March.

Across the path from the azaleas, behind the benches, are the two stately amur cork trees, *Phellodendron amurense,* with deeply ridged, soft bark mentioned by M. M. Graff. The common name amur refers to a river in the tree's native region in northeast Asia. Its botanical name, *Phellodendron,* comes from the Greek *phellos* (cork) and *dendron* (tree), though these are not the trees from which the corks in wine bottles are made. Wine bottle corks come from the cork oak, *Quercus suber,* an evergreen oak native to southern Europe. The reference to cork in the amur cork tree is to its soft, somewhat spongy bark. Amur cork trees also tolerate harsh urban conditions and supply tasty black fruit to generations of birds.

In winter months, bird feeders decorate the cork trees' branches with dangling, pendulous ornaments, many simply cut from plastic jugs fitted with bird-sized doorways. Some of these contraptions are topped with Frisbees to keep the squirrels out. Bird-watchers voluntarily tend these feeders, even on the most bone-chilling days, filling them with seed and making certain that the wintering birds will not want for food. The feeders, suspended from the branches, give a sense of cool surrealism, their plastic life-sustaining fruit bobbing on the leafless trees. Something deeply human settles over Azalea Pond in winter and realigns our spirit here in the Ramble, perhaps because of the fluttering, lively activity of both birds and bird-watchers. John Burroughs, preeminent nature observer, writer, and young friend of Walt Whitman, touches on this animal-human spirit in his 1905 essay, "The Ways of Nature":

> The ways of nature—who can map them, or fathom them, or interpret them, or do much more than read a

hint correctly here and there? Of one thing we may be pretty certain, namely, that the ways of wild nature may be studied in our human ways, inasmuch as the latter are an evolution from the other, till we come to the ethical code, to altruism and self-sacrifice. Here we seem to breathe another air, though probably this code differs no more from the animal standards of conduct than our physical atmosphere differs from that of early geologic time.

Many other native and non-native shrubs and trees, planted to accent the pond with color and texture, can be found on this short stretch along Azalea Pond. The first two trees on the southeast edge near the rustic bridge are red maples, *Acer rubrum,* with light-gray, moderately flaky bark and three to five lobed leaves. These were well placed by some landscape designer who appreciated the harmony of plant and environment. The red maple, also known as swamp maple, loves to have its roots wet. Some of the other trees and shrubs to look for include sorrel tree, viburnum, shadbush, barberry, five-leaf aralia, rhododendron, spicebush, swamp white oak, ironwood, catalpa, and Korean dogwood.

The side tour returns to the lake by retracing our steps to Azalea Pond. For the adventurous, an alternate route follows the path to the left of the bridge instead of recrossing it. The shallow stream will still be on your right as you follow the path around the large rock outcrop hillock. On the other side of the hillock, off to the left, is a restored rustic shelter, the only original one remaining of fifteen such structures used by nineteenth-century park visitors for shelter and rest. In 1982 the restoration crews of the Central Park Conservancy repaired this sole survivor to its present condition. Using the unique carpentry skills honed on this project, park restoration crews went on to restore and rebuild many more rustic structures, including the Cop Cot summerhouse, the first rustic shelter built in Central Park, visited on the 59th Street Pond Walk.

Continue along the path from where you left it for the rustic shelter and you'll return to the Gill, with Shadow Bridge across the water. The path now takes you left and down the steps to lamppost #7525 where this side tour began.

Continue along the path to the next rustic bridge, known as Gill Bridge (No. 21). Two small wooden rustic benches tucked into a niche of the rocky terrain near lamppost #7529 provide an opportunity to sit and enjoy the sounds of the cascading water from the rocks above. The bench and the bridge are often victims of graffiti vandals. Graffiti is synonymous with cities and its removal is as necessary to the aesthetic health of a park as its gardens. A complimentary nod to the Central Park Conservancy should be noted here, whether the bench is graffitoed or not. In the 1970s, Central Park had fallen into one of its worst periods of disrepair. Dead and dying vegetation swept over the park's landscapes. Its infrastructure decayed to the point where the drainage system broke down and floods were common. And graffiti everywhere accented the decay. It is to the credit and vision of the founders and planners of the Central Park Conservancy that one of their first priorities was to form a graffiti removal crew. The removal of graffiti, and keeping it removed whenever it appeared, demonstrated the Conservancy's commitment to restoring Central Park and maintaining it once restoration had begun. If a bench or bridge has been vandalized you may report it at the end of this tour by calling (212) 628-1036.

On the other side of the bridge, at the head of the stairs, the path divides right and left. The rounded alcove, with the large rock outcrop behind it, once held the sculpted bust of Johann Christopher Friederich von Schiller, eighteenth-century German playwright, poet, and essayist and one of the leading literary figures of the time. In 1859 his bust was the first piece of sculpture placed in the park, presented by the city's German popula-

Shagbark hickory

tion to honor the centennial of Schiller's 1759 birthdate. The bust can now be seen on the northern end of the Mall, mid-park at the line of 71st Street, where it was moved in 1953.

The walk continues along the path to the left. Twenty feet past lamppost #7533, on your left stop and savor a rare find in Central Park, the shagbark hickory, *Carya ovata*. Of the four species of hickory in the park this one can never be mistaken for the others. Notice the gray bark splitting into long strips or plates, giving it a shaggy appearance. *The 1857 Catalogue of Plants in Central Park* lists five hundred specimens of shagbark hickory. *The 1982 Tree Inventory* listed only five shagbark hickories. Since then dozens of seeds, seedlings, and small balled-and-burlapped shagbarks have been planted, mostly in the woodlands, in the hopes of reestablishing the species.

Move on to where the paths divide at lamppost #7635. The tour follows the pipe rail on the left to the top of a steep incline where there is a restoration in progress. This small area was the first chosen for Ramble landscape restoration by the Woodlands Advisory Board. At this writing the area is surrounded by a fence that protects its various erosion-control techniques and plantings. The plants selected for the project were chosen for endurance more than beauty. White wood aster and snake-root were selected for the ground cover because these tough native plants establish quickly and tolerate harsh urban conditions. The restorers of this landscape, from the managers to the Woodlands Advisory Board to the crew members who pounded the stakes for erosion control and planted the asters, hope their efforts will be appreciated by the user public. If this project succeeds, the surrounding hillocks and slopes will be under restoration in the near future.

To take a quick and somewhat precipitous tour to the Cave, follow the pipe rail fence around the steps on the right of lamppost #7623A. If you duck through the railing you will discover the old stone stairs that lead to the mortared wall that seals off the Cave. Olmsted and Vaux created the Cave by closing off a large fissure between two rock outcrops with large boulders. A platform allowed boats to dock and boaters to enter the cave from the cove below. This opening to the Cave and another found on the other side of the stone arch were closed in the 1920s after the Cave was deemed unsafe for casual use. It's a pity, as this unique feature provided an incomparable spelunking adventure found nowhere else in the park's overall design.

Back on the path, follow the pipe rail to the end and head left down toward the water. Along the way, survey the cove for some moisture-loving plants such as blue-flag and yellow irises flowering in late June with their long, lanceolate leaves, like a fountain of small spears. Also look for sensitive fern, with its light-green, distinctive fern foliage; it is the only fern that regenerates regularly in the park and was once favored by the Iroquois Indians for the edible rootstock. Look for butter-cups, whose botanical name *Ranunculus* refers to frogs, indicating its suitability to wet areas. The blue bugle, with a small spire of blue flowers in spring, is considered by many horti-culturists to be a weed but is welcomed here for its diversity and ability to tolerate shade. Solomon's seal, an indicator of fertile woodlands, arches up gracefully with long, oval leaves and small, dangling flowers in late spring. And several species of aster thrive here, their small daisylike flowers mostly white to bluish, prominent in autumn.

The cove contains one of the few consistently favorable natural habitats for moisture-loving plants in the park. The soil remains moist throughout the year and the diffused light is adequate for many species of flowering plants. The fertile soil (actually the eroded topsoil from the higher slopes) is replete with nutrients, and the wet, mucky conditions discourage trampling. Because the cove receives little foot traffic, some ground-nesting birds, most often mallard ducks, tuck their nests into the shore here with little interference from humans. Dogs, on the other hand, allowed to run free by inconsiderate owners, are not deterred by the muddy conditions; they disturb the ducks and destroy their nests.

Beyond the end of the pipe rail where the paths diverge, bear left along the path skirting the water. At the water's edge two large, double-trunk, blackhaw viburnum, *Viburnum prunifolium,* dip into the Lake. The blackhaw, also known as wild raisin, will be encountered and discussed at length on the East Lake Walk. To the right of the blackhaws a view opens up to the south. Pause a moment to enjoy this spectacular skyline vista of Central Park South and Central Park West over the Lake. This spot was designed to enthrall visitors and transport them out of the city by using the city itself as the vehicle of escape.

Continue on along the path to the pipe rail, following it up the hill. At the next intersection of paths, the tour continues left and crosses the overpass known formally as the High Rustic Arch (discussed farther along). At the next intersection, two large Chinese scholar trees, *Sophora japonica,* on the right across from lamppost #7703, arch widely into the canopy with brownish bark and compound leaves. Scholar trees, because their canopies can spread out to seventy-five feet from the main trunk, have been cultivated for many centuries to decorate Asian temples.

Again, bear to the left and down the stairs, which are lined with arrowwood viburnum, *Viburnum dentatum,* on the right. At the bottom of the steps, bear left toward Bank Rock Bridge. But before crossing the bridge take a moment to investigate the High Rustic Arch by following the path as it swings left to where the arch rises between the buttresses of natural rock. Its primitive appeal is not unlike encountering the remains of an ancient civilization in an unexplored jungle. The arch contrasts with more formal architectural structures found in the park, yet its crude design fits comfortably into the scheme of the Ramble.

Return to Bank Rock Bridge, which was named for the steep rocks that rise—or bank up to the east—and crosses Bank Rock Bay. Originally this bridge was named Oak Bridge for the finely constructed balustrade and posts crafted of cast iron and white oak with footboards of yellow pine. Years of neglect brought it to its present state: a 60-foot-long, 15-foot-wide, nondescript connection between the two banks, constructed of steel rails and ordinary wooden planks. Its utility is indisputable, but it has no affinity to the original Oak Bridge's charm as a portal to the Ramble.

Many bird-watching regulars begin their sojourn in the Ramble from Bank Rock Bridge, meeting early in the morning with hope of spotting the waterfowl in the bay before continuing on to search for warblers and other interior species. The protected bay to the north of the bridge offers sustenance and protection to many of the birds that breed and feed in the park. In a tree on the northwest bank of the bay a pair of green herons, *Butorides virescens,* successfully nested in 1994. The appeal of birds that only occasionally nest in Central Park—herons, swans, hawks, etc.—reaches beyond bird-watchers. To some extent we are all naturalists, torn between development of the land and protection of it. Any successful venture of nature, such as breeding birds or the reemergence of threatened species, gives us hope that nature is not losing ground but regaining it.

On the other side of the bridge, keep the water on your left and proceed south along the footpath past the water fountain until you reach Balcony Bridge on West Drive overlooking the Lake. Balcony Bridge receives its name from the two inset balconies with stone benches on its west side overlooking the Lake, Fifth Avenue, and Central Park South. Once again we enjoy a spectacular view of the Manhattan skyline over the placid Lake. This section of West Drive terminated the original Winter Drive, a stretch heavily planted with evergreen trees and shrubs, which began at approximately 100th Street. Winter Drive is discussed more fully on the 100th Street Pool Walk.

At the first traffic light the base of a burly turkey oak, *Quercus cerris,* is overtaking the curb. Follow the pipe rail on the left to the next traffic light. On lamppost #7507 a sign indicates our arrival at Hernshead, a small promontory with a rock outcrop jutting into the Lake named for its slight resemblance to a heron. "Hern" is an archaic pronunciation of heron, a bird not uncommon in Central Park, but not common at Hernshead, where too much human activity discourages their presence.

Proceed forward toward the water. On the right an area encircled with more pipe rail displays some diverse vegetation. Look for Virginia bluebells, *Mertensia virginica,* in April; ephemerals with pink and blue bell-shaped flowers that disappear by June; a large stand of mayapple, *Podophyllum peltatum,* recognized by its two large fan-lobed, umbrellalike leaves, a rare herbaceous ephemeral in Central Park that in the wild forms huge colonies; the shrubby barberry, *Berberis* sp., easily recognized by its thorns and small yellow flowers in late April to early May; several azaleas, low-growing, semi-evergreen to deciduous shrubs with small clustered leaves and distinctive, brilliantly colored white and pink blossoms in early May; a number of ferns, again uncommon in the park out of protected spots such as this; snakeroot; and asters.

Continue along to the Ladies Pavilion straight ahead. This rustic structure was originally designed by Jacob Wrey Mould in 1871 and served as a bus shelter at Columbus Circle until 1913. After falling into disrepair it was moved here and fully restored in the 1980s.

Keeping the water on your left, cross over the stepping-stones at the edge of the water to the main path leading to the smaller rustic shelter. A number of both moisture-loving and drier plants enhance this water's edge, including blue flag iris; phlox, with five outspread pale violet or whitish petals; New England aster, a late-summer beauty, the park's showiest wild aster with deep violet blossoms crowning the five-to-seven-foot stalk; daisy fleabane, an asterlike wildflower blooming early in the summer with up to a hundred rays on the magenta and pink flowers; black-eyed Susan, easily one of the all-time favorites of garden and meadow; and cup-plant, a tall sun-flowerlike plant with large winglike leaves and three-to-five-inch yellow blossoms.

From here we'll move along to our next destination, Wagner's Cove and Cherry Hill. Across the drive to the west notice the steep slope rising up to Strawberry Fields. At any time of year this slope and all of Strawberry Fields displays attractive colors and textures with ferns, wildflowers, shrubs, and trees. Strawberry Fields was donated to Central Park by Yoko Ono in memory of John Lennon, after his assassination in 1980.

About halfway to Wagner's Cove, at lamppost #7239, a path veers left to a rustic shelter on the water and opens to a prominent view across the Lake to the Ramble and Bow

Bridge. This secluded spot, surrounded by dense, thorny vegetation, is a pleasing place to contemplate the Lake for its own sake, as all the water bodies in the park possess their own characteristic plant and animal life. Here in early summer the Lake often has a tie-dyed green color, giving it an artificial appearance caused by both green and blue-green algae.

The deep, rich color is caused in part by high levels of phosphorus, which is added to New York City's drinking water in the form of calcium orthophosphate by the Department of Environmental Protection. The calcium coats the water conduits throughout the city and protects the water from leaching copper and lead, found in many of the older pipes. However, the phosphorus also enters the park's water system that feeds the aquatic plants. This creates a tremendous imbalance in the ecology of the water bodies by raising water temperatures and depleting oxygen, which leads to periodic fish kills during hot summer months. Efforts are made to maintain temperature and oxygen balance by keeping water levels higher during critical periods. When the water temperature rises above 85 degrees, fire hydrants are opened to supply cold, oxygenated water to the lakes and ponds. The Lake and Harlem Meer suffer most from these problems because of their large surface area, lack of shade, and shallow water. When the overabundant algae die by midsummer the result is a muddy, brown-colored water, which is caused by the algaes' microscopic corpses.

Continue back along the path to the arbor (known in Central Park as a pergola), which by mid-April is massed with clusters of purple wisteria blossoms. This is one of four restored pergolas in the park. Wagner's Cove begins farther ahead where the row of benches ends. The path bends around the head of the Cove, passing an array of silky dogwood, English ivy, periwinkle, ferns, tulips, and a series of hemlocks along the water's edge, all planted during the 1993 restoration of Wagner's Cove. This is mostly a decorative landscape, with more thought given to its aesthetic appearance and stability than to its wetland environment.

Follow the curve of the path around and up the hill to the old carriage parking area known in the nineteenth century as the Cherry Hill Concourse, a convenient and practical gathering place for early park carriage users. The large fountain in the center of the paved circle was a watering trough for horses. The name Cherry Hill refers to the numerous flowering cherry trees, *Prunus serrulata,* prominent here in spring with their puffy pink and white flowers.

On the left a stone path veers down to the water and leads to a rustic shelter. At the top of these stairs and along the path a number of stunning, diversely colored azaleas blossom in May. A plaque attached to a boulder at the foot of the stairs dedicates this cove landscape to Robert Wagner, mayor of New York from 1954 to 1965.

Back at the top of the stairs follow the path left until it veers off toward the water. At the beginning of this path a unique European cutleaf beech spreads out and heavily shades the ground beneath it. The root system radiates from the trunk like a spidery elephant's foot. Nothing grows beneath the branches, typical of the beech's dominance, but the azaleas surrounding the beech form a dense and comely stand.

On the lawn area to the right, a number of old Japanese flowering cherry trees, prominent with their dark bark and showy blossoms, provide shade, beauty, and grace to yet another dramatic view over the Lake. On sunny weekend afternoons the lawn is often spread over with blankets topped with picnickers enjoying the shade of the trees in summer and its blossoms in April. Entertainers occasionally perform for the crowd from the walk near the water.

The walk ends directly ahead at Bow Bridge.

East Lake Walk

East Drive at 75th Street

THE WALK BEGINS at Loeb Boathouse with the parking lot on your right and the iron gates of the restaurant on your left. Along the way we'll encounter several glacial boulder deposits, a rustic boat landing, Bow Bridge (a favorite park water span), Bethesda Terrace, and some of Central Park's favorite bird-watching spots deep in the Ramble.

On the right of the path, two young willow oaks, *Quercus phellos,* form a portal to the cobblestone footpath entrance to the parking lot. The oaks are recognized by their slightly furrowed gray bark, linear leaves, and drooping lower branches. Beyond the willow oaks, on the right, an old, dignified red maple, *Acer rubrum,* and a younger red maple a bit farther up on the left stand as sentinels at this entrance to the Ramble. The two maples are varieties of the same species encountered on the 100th Street Pool Walk, differing only in the colors of their flowers, seeds, and autumnal leaves. The larger tree on the right displays crimson flowers in spring, then equally colorful seeds in fall, while the younger maple on the left displays

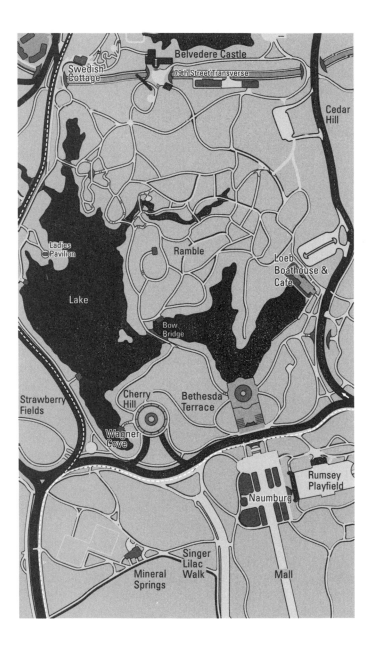

Belvedere Castle

Swedish Cottage

79th Street Transverse

Cedar Hill

Ladies Pavilion

Ramble

Loeb Boathouse & Cafe

Lake

Bow Bridge

Strawberry Fields

Cherry Hill

Bethesda Terrace

Wagner Cove

Rumsey Playfield

Naumburg

Mineral Springs

Singer Lilac Walk

Mall

flowers and leaves with an orange-yellow tinge. Plant nurseries breed dozens of red maple varieties for their seasonal color, then bestow descriptive varietal names on them such as Autumn Flame, October Glory, Red Sunset, and Northwood.

Red maple

On the right, across the path from the younger maple, five American hackberries, *Celtis occidentalis,* with light-gray, knobby bark, surround a large boulder. Hackberries, found in abundance in the Ramble, frequently regenerate in the Central Park landscape, especially in their preferred niche around craggy, rock-strewn slopes. Under ideal conditions, in bottomlands and along rivers, hackberries can grow to five feet in diameter and one hundred feet tall. The tallest hackberry in Central Park was nearly eighty feet in height until a severe storm in 1992 blew it down; a sixty-foot hackberry will be seen later on this walk.

As you approach the fence, on the left a large pin oak, *Quercus palustris,* a boulder at its base, welcomes visitors to this eastern entrance of the Ramble. Considered by many to be the heart of Central Park, the Ramble is one of three woodland areas in the park. The others are North Woods, explored in the Loch Walk and Hallett Sanctuary, visited on the 59th Street Pond Walk.

Where the paths branch off in three directions, bear left along the fence. The fence is a barrier against park users who would otherwise cause desire paths through the turf, as has happened at the other end of this fence. Upkeep of fences, many torn down by inconsiderate park users, is one of the most time-consuming tasks of Central Park's maintenance crews.

Along the right edge of the path, an area of scrubby vegetation flourishes, dominated by black cherry trees interspersed with hackberries and an herbaceous cover of woodland aster. This is the first of many rough, unmanicured locations to be encountered in the Ramble, which constitutes 36 of the 130 acres of woodland in Central Park.

Because the Ramble lies in the center of the park—a sea of green away from its concrete shores—many generations of birds have flocked here to hunt and peck for food on their migratory routes. The Audubon Society ranks the Ramble among the top fifteen bird-watching locations in the United States. For some people the attraction to bird-watching is not fully understood, but to dedicated bird-watchers the reasons are clear, as it involves several human emotions as well as certain ineffable thrills. In their comprehensive book, *A Guide to Bird Behavior* (volume 2), Donald and Lillian Stokes explain it this way:

> The behavior of birds can be divided into two broad categories: maintenance behavior and social behavior. The former includes all actions a bird does to maintain itself, such as preening, feeding, bathing, and so on. The latter includes all interactions between birds, such as courtship, territoriality, breeding, flocking. . . . Social behavior is one of the most exciting aspects of birds and one that has often been neglected. In social behavior, one individual is coordinating its life and

actions with those of another, and this always involves communication of some kind, either in fixed sounds or gestures or in general movement patterns. This struggle to connect separate lives is common to all animal life, and we find that through watching it we have become more aware of its importance in the lives of all animals.

Before moving on to the end of the fence, turn your attention up the slope about thirty feet to the large, split-rock outcrop with a small boulder wedged into it. This boulder was possibly placed there by the Wisconsin glacier. We'll examine this phenomenon farther along in the tour.

Toward the end of the fence look to the right side of the path for a stand of mock orange, *Philadelphus* sp., recognized by its scraggly shrubbiness, its flaky, light-tan bark with egg-shaped, toothed leaves and opposite branches and a prominent display of creamy white flowers in May and June. Mock orange was planted abundantly throughout the park earlier this century and, though not planted in recent decades, still flourishes in many areas. The flowers are fragrant and attractive, but when not in flower the plant offers little more than this leggy hedge effect. Most of the mock orange shrubs in Central Park are hybrids native to Asia Minor, introduced to the gardens around the world in the sixteenth century. The genus name *Philadelphus,* given for unknown reasons by Linnaeus, is for Ptolemy Philadelphus, king of Egypt, 283–247 B.C.

At the end of the fence turn around to look back along the path. Notice that where the paths fork a woodsy, pastoral view rolls through the trees. As the landscape rises the paths disappear into the dense greenery. The paths in the Ramble were designed to convey the effect of a meandering stroll through a country woodlot. Though the Ramble encompasses a mere 3 percent of Central Park's 843 acres, it is possible to walk in circles and not see the same place twice. Many tourists unacquainted with the Ramble do get lost here. But on this tour we'll follow the edge of the Lake, keeping the water on the left.

Farther along the path, past the edge of the fence, on the left examine the five-leaf aralia, *Acanthopanax sieboldianus,* a low, dense, non-native thorny barrier planting recognized by its light-green, five-leaflet foliage and its small thorns. This rapidly spreading Japanese native protects the slope along the edge of the path from foot traffic. It was planted here in the early 1980s and has successfully prevented park users from trampling the slope that leads down to the Lake.

American hackberry

Beyond the five-leaf aralia the paths diverge again. Notice the two pin oaks accenting the entrance to the path on the right. This common landscaping device follows the tradition of classical landscape designers who used plants to accent entrances and structures. We encountered this device on the Loch Walk at the path to Spring Banks Arch and again at the Huddlestone Bridge. Follow this path through the pin oak portal to the top of the knoll where hackberries and mock orange dominate the vegetation.

At the top of the knoll you can examine the split boulder from the row of benches that lines the crest. Notice the contrasted color and smoother texture of the smaller, rounded boulder inside the split outcrop. The glacier may have carried the smaller boulder to this spot and, like a clamming knife opening a clam, wedged it into the crevice of the outcrop. It is also possible that the outcrop was split long before the glaciers arrived, however, and that the designers of the park saw an opportunity to place the boulder there for this effect. Unfortunately, no records indicate where the designers placed boulders or where the glacier placed them. When touring the Ramble we need to keep in mind that the pre-park landscape was often altered by adding soil to some locations and by rearranging and dynamiting rock outcrops to produce picturesque effects.

Return to the divergent paths for a side tour along the unpaved path across from the pin oaks. This path leads to the Point, a finger-shaped peninsula jutting into the Lake toward Bethesda Terrace. Olmsted and Vaux landscaped the Point with wetland and heath (*Ericaceous*) plant species such as black alder, mountain laurel, rhododendron, Spanish oak, and spirea, which have since succumbed to age and pedestrian traffic. An attempt was made in the early 1980s to restore the Point by preventing park users from trampling the slopes that lead toward the water (for more restoration detail, see the West Lake Walk). The designers at that time installed a thicket composed of many non-native thorny shrubs to deter trampling, but the plan backfired. The dense planting actually encouraged more trampling, because certain user groups, seeking isolation, found refuge in the thick cover. Now a number of illegitimate, single-file footpaths trail down the slope from the legitimate gravel path.

Twenty paces past the black iron railing the path opens out on the right to a large rock outcrop overlooking the Lake. The densely vegetated cove below is the Willow Oven. From this splendid vantage point on the rock outcrop you can enjoy a wide view of the Lake toward the horizon, while at the same time appreciate the expanse of woodland on the far shore. Below this outcrop, at the water's edge, a single black willow, *Salix nigra,* part of the overall stand of trees in the Willow Oven, leans out over the Lake. This black willow and the other willows off to the right give the Willow Oven the first part of its name. The "oven" alludes to the warmth generated by the sun's heat as it is refracted off the water, which increases heat caught below the canopy and raises the temperature of the cove by a degree or two.

Across the water to the left a dense stand of an aggressive alien weed, *Phragmites communis,* sways in the wind along the bank. Described in the 59th Street Pond Walk, phragmites have replaced other more attractive water-loving grasses. Notice the plant's curvilinear growth into the water, an indication that they are spreading outward from the shore. Phragmites are periodically dredged from most of the park's water bodies, but less so in the Ramble as debates rage over their importance to a few species of birds and dragonflies. Until an alternative wetland plant is agreed upon, the phragmites will continue their advance into the Lake.

Near the water below the rock outcrop, a number of burrows disappear under the rocks. These are home to a few of the Ramble's groundhogs, also popularly known as woodchucks, *Marmota monax,* a number of which inhabit the park, although no official head count exists. Groundhogs, in the same family as squirrels, *Sciuridae,* are the largest wild rodent in the park and are sometimes mistaken for rats. Unlike rats, they are much preferred by naturalists and nature lovers, who favor any wildlife in the park that do not depend upon people or garbage for sustenance. The herbivorous groundhog feeds on the succulent shoots of newly planted shrubs and wildflowers in springtime, which occasionally creates problems in the gardens and newly planted landscapes. Fortunately, groundhogs hibernate through the winter and do not, like rabbits, which don't hibernate, eat the terminal winter buds of newly planted seedlings.

Continue to the end of the Point to enjoy a view of Bethesda Terrace, across the Lake on the left, reflected on the water. Details of the terrace, its fountain, and a bit of history will be provided farther along on this walk. If it's a warm, sunny weekend scores of people will be enjoying the Terrace. On the other edge of the point to the west a unique vista encompasses Bow Bridge, crossed later on this walk.

On the return trip off the Point, take a moment to identify a few of the shrubs and trees that line the dirt path. Look for yellow barberry, a small shrub recognized by its small leaves and thorns tucked close to the stems; black jetbead, with its opposite leaves positioned like wings and showy white blossoms in early May that turn to jet black, beady fruit in autumn; shrub dogwood, discussed at length on the Turtle Pond Walk; and multiflora rose, with small, tight foliage and many small rose blossoms in mid-June. The dominant trees on the Point are black locust and black cherry, two species that colonize disturbed landscapes.

Return to the paved path and continue past the bench on the right where another path intersects. Across from the bench

Black locust

one particularly admirable sixty-foot-high hackberry graces the Ramble. Mature specimens of hackberry are rare in Central Park. *The 1982 Tree Inventory* lists 379 hackberries, but most of those are less than thirty feet high. Hackberries occasionally reach a hundred feet tall in their preferred habitat of rich, alluvial soil in the Ohio Valley. This park specimen is fortunate to have its roots anchored in an underground spring, which can be seen in spring and fall flowing over the path and emptying into the Willow Oven.

Thirty feet beyond the hackberry to the left a ridge overlooks the Lake through Willow Oven where you can stand poised over one of the premier bird-watching sites in the park. The cove below has gained international attention from bird-watchers for the many bird species that find their way here to forage in the protected copse of willow, aster, elderberry, and ash. Even during nonmigrating seasons, nature watchers gather at this strategic vantage point to observe birds scratching under the vegetation, turtles basking on logs, and groundhogs in the boulders across the water.

Along the shoreline of Willow Oven many species of wetland plants can be observed. In the spring of 1995, because the area was slowly degrading to phragmites and siltation, a stabilization of Willow Oven commenced with the cooperation and counsel of the naturalists and bird-watchers who frequent the Ramble. Without intervention, the Oven would have become a silted-in pocket of phragmite lacking the diverse vegetation that attracts the wildlife which makes it notable. A small but spreading patch of phragmite was replaced with native sedges, rushes, wetland wildflowers, and a shrub willow species. The phragmites continue to be contained in the Oven, but only time, which means many years in ecological restoration, will determine whether the project is successful.

Farther along the path, near the water and before the path bends off to the right, one of the few large pin oaks in the park with sweeping lower branches intact, stands unpruned and vigorous near the water. Notice how the lower branches swoop down from the sides appearing fancifully like the tutu of a pirouetting ballerina. The pin oak's placement near the water contributes to this tree's vigor, as pin oaks naturally occur in bottomlands in moist woods. In 1857, before construction of the park began, Ignatious Pilat, an influential botanist of the time, and Charles Rawolle, a fellow botanist, compiled the *Catalogue of Plants in the Terrain of Central Park,* listing 281 tree, shrub, and herbaceous species. The pin oak was listed in the catalogue along with nine other oak species. Of the pin oak, the catalogue says, "A very handsome and middle-sized tree, with light and elegant foliage, to be found mostly in low grounds." Elsewhere in the park, the lower branches of pin oaks are pruned off because they are potential eyesores. They remain on this tree because pruning live branches in the Ramble is rarely done, except for safety purposes; to be injured by this tree one must leave the path, which, with few exceptions, is against the rules.

Pin oak

Farther ahead another path veers off to the right up a small hill. Across from that path another large pin oak, with only a remnant of its tutu, thrives along the edge of the water. A bit beyond that take a moment to inspect the large boulder near the water before the rustic shelter. This is obviously not a glacial erratic; yet a hundred years ago we would not judge so quickly. The smaller rocks, which can now be seen supporting the boulder, were then covered with soil to increase its lofty appeal. Boulders played major roles in the original design of the park, and many were positioned for design effects or, as mentioned, to give the impression of being glacial erratics. Some, like this large one, were raised on smaller stones to be prominent against the far shoreline and tree canopy. But years of unchecked storm water streaming down the slope from behind eroded the soil that covered the smaller stones, diminishing the lofty effect and leaving this fabricated effect. The soil that covered the smaller rocks, and much more soil from up the slope, now forms a silted buffer between the boulder and the Lake.

Examine the large boulder closely. Notice that a small crack, or fissure, runs through the center connecting it to a smaller fissure. These fissures, together with the tapered shape of the boulder, resemble a smirking dinosaur's head with its face looking off toward the water. In 1993, an imaginative graffitist took advantage of this arrangement and painted in the eyes, nose, and smirk of the dinosaur, all of which was promptly removed by the Central Park Conservancy's graffiti crew.

A few feet beyond the rustic boat landing, the paths intersect. Before following the path to the left take a moment to examine the bottlebrush buckeye, *Aesculus parviflora,* a four-to-six-foot shrub with palmate leaves located on the right of the intersection, growing between two London plane trees. This native shrub, rare in the park, acquired its common name from its flowers, which in the first week of July are tapered wands resembling a bottlebrush rocketing up from the center of dark green, palmate leaves. The shrub's botanical name means "mast-bearing tree with small flowers," a deceiving description as the flowers are quite prominent en masse, though individual flowers are quite small.

The bottlebrush buckeye's native habitat occurs farther south and west to Kentucky, but it has adapted well in its limited locations in Central Park. It is related by genus to the horse chestnut, which is encountered on several other walks, but unlike the horse chestnut, bottlebrush buckeye produces little fruit at this latitude. In the South it is known to produce abundant, edible nuts. Perhaps in the future, if the global warming scenario is realized, New Yorkers will have bottlebrush buckeye nuts roasting over an open fire, but until that time we have its attractive flowers and unique form to complement the American garden in the Ramble.

To the right, across the path from an unnumbered lamppost, several American sycamores form a small stand, with a few mottled yellow-barked London plane trees sprinkled in. The sycamores are distinguished from the London plane by their whiter bark, which is raised at the base in small plates. A glance into the sycamore's crown reveals the "witch's broom" effect—so called because of the gnarled branches at the top—caused by *Anthracnose,* a fungus disease of the buds and twigs that causes erratic angular branching, but is rarely fatal to the tree.

Continue along the path toward the bridge. At left between the boulder and the bridge, the tall, gangly shrub with coarse tan bark, elliptical or egg-shaped small leaves with fine-teethed edges is blackhaw viburnum, *Viburnum prunifolium.* Through the second and third week of May this native shrub will be covered with clusters of mildly fragrant white flowers that in September through October become small blackish fruits, often referred to as wild raisins. Wildlife such as fox, bobwhite, and many songbirds eat the fruit and, while a bit tart, it is sometimes collected as a wild food by humans, though picking is discouraged as well as illegal in Central Park.

Blackhaw, which continues to be planted in the park, is listed in the 1857 catalogue of plants as "very numerous" and "very handsome in flower and foliage." Today, many urban parks favor the planting of native plant species, including blackhaw, although not to the exclusion of non-native ornamentals, if the non-natives are not invasive. In the last decade the use of native plants in landscape design has entered the environmental movement, as observed by William K. Stevens, in his book on ecological restoration, *Miracle Under the Oaks:*

> There is a widespread view among veteran conserva-
> tionists . . . that the human population explosion will
> roll over the rest of the natural world unimpeded
> before expending its momentum in the next century
> or two, and that every patch of viable habitat is there-
> fore precious. If enough arks can be built, main-
> tained, and kept afloat on the human tide, there will
> be enough raw material left once the flood subsides to
> "reclothe the earth."

Even though Stevens's statement is somewhat bleak, it does consider at least a partial solution to our concerns about the environment. Many young landscape designers begin their careers in urban parks, where the salaries are low but the experience is rewarding. The conviction to foster native plants has been built into the curriculum of many schools of land-scape design, and designers bring this conviction to urban parks by incorporating restoration ecology into their designs.

Move on to Bow Bridge. From the center of the bridge a broad vista unfolds, exposing the skylines of Fifth Avenue and Central Park West. On Central Park West, toward the right, the prominent Dakota Apartments, designed and built in the early 1880s by Henry J. Hardenbergh, complements the park's landscape with its bold architecture. On the northwest corner of the bridge, a handsome stand of black locust trees, with their sweet fragrance in early June, weaves into the sky. To the east, in mid-April, splashes of sunflower-yellow forsythia adorn the banks of the Point before the dense foliage of trees and shrubs appear throughout the thirty-six acres of contiguous Ramble woodlands.

Toward the end of April and through the summer, rowboats dominate the Lake. The rowing style of the less experienced boaters mimics the circular courtship ritual of the mallard ducks in spring and the spiral swimming patterns of other dabbling ducks such as the shovelers, *Spatula clypeata,* that feed on the Lake in late autumn. From beneath the bridge, the cooing of pigeons sitting on nests or staying out of the wind emanates hauntingly through the slatted floorboards. Bird-watchers treasure Bow Bridge for its panoramic opportunity to watch for migrating waterfowl such as the wood ducks, canvasbacks, pintails, teals, and many others. A visit to the Ramble would seem incomplete without a visit to Bow Bridge, which often leaves visitors with a favorable experience of Manhattan.

Bow Bridge was designed by Calvert Vaux and Jacob Wrey Mould, and constructed in 1862. The ornamentation is consistent with their style of using Gothic cinquefoils, abstract foliage, and interlaced spirals to embellish the railings and balustrades. The four corners were originally adorned with large flower vases. As practical portage with a view, the bridge is unsurpassed in the park. The 15-foot-8-inch-wide bridge spans 142 feet from bank to bank and arches 9 feet 6 inches above the Lake. In 1974, after more than a century of exposure to the elements, the eroding bridge was restored.

On the bridge's southeast corner a thicket of silky dogwood, *Cornus amomum,* thrives near the water as it would if encountered in the wild. The flowers, white or pink flat-topped clusters, closely resemble those of the viburnums. The fruits are small drupes, about half the size of a wild cherry, with pulp covering a solid pit. The common name, dogwood, has nothing to do with dogs. The Europeans used the hardwood of these shrubs as skewers for meat and called it "dagwood" from the old English *dag,* meaning a dagger or sharp object.

Turn to the southwest corner of the bridge for an examination of a leatherleaf viburnum, *Viburnum rhytidophyllum,* named for its thick leaves, which are unlike any other viburnum in the park. If you touch a leaf you'll find the texture to be similar to that of raw leather. Its coarse habit and dark color are useful in spacious park landscapes, where it does not overwhelm other more subtle ornamentals. Left of the leatherleaf viburnum, a more delicate viburnum graces the end of the bridge. This Koreanspice viburnum, *Viburnum carlessi,* would be welcome on any size property. In late April and early May the blossoms emit a splendid, spicy fragrance.

The path to the right leads to Cherry Hill, a diversely planted landscape that we'll visit on the West Lake Walk. On the southwest corner of these intersecting paths, a large stand of Japanese barberry, *Berberis thunbergii,* spreads out on the lawn. Commonly planted in the park as an ornamental for its petite and colorful foliage, barberry forms a formidable hedge with dense thorns. A native barberry, *B. canadensis,* grows in dry woodlands but does not have the ornamental appeal of the Japanese barberry. Although it makes a fine barrier hedge, the aggressive Japanese barberry invades open native ecosystems. Its seeds, eaten and spread by many songbirds, have found their way out of gardens and parks to inhabit abandoned pastures and woodland edges, where they displace and threaten the diversity of our native vegetation.

Continue along the path toward Bethesda Terrace. Along the way several clusters of Koreanspice viburnum enhance the vista across the Lake to the Ramble, Loeb Boathouse, and Fifth Avenue. Other well-ordered placements of lakeside plantings complement this walk, including large tulip trees, oaks, and elms separating various ornamental shrubs. Other attractive landscape plants are the native cranberry viburnum, *Viburnum triloba,* with its maple-shaped, three-lobed leaves and whorls of large, creamy white blossoms in mid-May; a variety of the native inkberry, *Ilex glabra compacta,* with compact, small evergreen leaves, tucked into some Korean-spice viburnum; the Southeast Asian winged euonymous, *Euonymous alatus,* with opposite, corklike small wings along the branches and red-tinged foliage; and a series of four magnolias at the entrance to the esplanade of Bethesda Terrace.

Bethesda Fountain, the centerpiece of the terrace, topped by the magnificent sculpture *Angel of the Waters,* attracts visitors from around the world and is arguably the most photographed ornament in Central Park. On almost any pleasant weekday, film crews will be found positioning models from one vantage point or another with the fountain, terrace, Lake, and Ramble as backdrop. On weekends street entertainers gather to perform to the delight of crowds, while young in-line skaters test their mettle on the steep stairs, much to the chagrin of the Parks Enforcement Patrol (PEP) officers. Many tourists and residents alike come just to sit and listen to the sounds of one of New York City's largest fountains.

The fountain, placed here in 1873, was sculpted by Emma Stebbins, the first woman sculptor to be commissioned for a work in New York City. *Angel of the Waters,* besides being a centerpiece for the park, also symbolizes the purity of New York's water. The fountain is fed by water from the Croton Aqueduct, opened in 1842 to bring fresh water to the citizens of New York from the Catskill Mountains. Prior to the Croton system, city water was plagued by infectious diseases brought on by the overburdened aquifer below Manhattan

Island, which prompted the construction of the upstate system. The story of the angel originates from the Gospel of Saint John in the New Testament, where an angel stepped into a pool in Jerusalem and after stepping out the water possessed healing powers. The image translates wholesomely through the centuries to a burgeoning city with newly acquired pure water.

The Esplanade, including the steps, the colorfully tiled area around the fountain, and the large, open corridor under the 72nd Street Transverse Road was designed by Jacob Wrey Mould and Calvert Vaux and received accolades from critics. The details of the sculptural work ornamenting the balustrades and endposts express motifs of nature and time. Amazingly, no two ornaments are repeated throughout Bethesda Terrace. The details of the miniature sculptures, even though somewhat worn by time, are meticulous.

Unfortunately, much of the fountain and terrace fell into disrepair over the years. The fountain ceased to flow, the miniatures were vandalized, the ceiling tiles in the corridor were cracked or missing, and the vegetation suffered from neglect. The terrace and fountain were closed off in the mid-1980s, restored, and reopened in 1987. That they still function over a decade later and through four administrative changes is a testament to the commitment of the Parks Department and the Central Park Conservancy to an enduring Central Park. As put by Marianne Cramer, the Central Park planner, "Bethesda Terrace is a testament in stone to the living park that surrounds it."

Across the esplanade the path leads to Loeb Boathouse. For a short side tour take the path on the right, across from lamppost #7324, to a rustic bench tucked away amid the rhododendrons. The four-to-eight-foot-high rhododendrons can be recognized by their thick evergreen foliage and vivid display of pink and white splashy flowers, which blossom in late May through early June. Passing through the pine trees and hemlocks of this evergreen corridor one can imagine strolling along a cool country lane. At the crest of this walk an ornate rustic bench invites the stroller to sit and rest. The bench, designed and built by Central Park Conservancy staff, was placed here in 1994. The wood for it, black locust, was gathered from Pelham Bay Park after a 1992 storm leveled more than a thousand black locust trees there. The same trees were used to construct the rustic rail encountered on the Loch Walk. Before being placed here this bench had a two-month-long stay at the Cooper-Hewitt Museum's rustic furniture exhibit.

Return to the tour route and at the next intersection of paths take the path down the steps. This path leads under the East Drive by way of Trefoil Arch, so named for the cloverlike design of the arch's east entrance. Even though Trefoil is a more lyrical name for the bridge, the Department of Trans-

Yellowthroat

portation (DOT) knows it as No. 2246170, seen on the green DOT tag on the southwest wall. The DOT assigns numbers to all the bridges in New York, including the tunnels and arches of the parks that pass under roadways. DOT numbers are citywide and differ from Olmsted and Vaux's bridge numbers. On the other side of the arch a rolling landscape carries us to the Conservatory Water where that tour begins at Fifth Avenue and 72nd Street.

Return to the path, where the tour ends back at Loeb Boathouse with some refreshment.

Conservatory Water Walk

Conservatory Water,
Fifth Avenue and 72nd Street

BEGIN THE WALK by entering Central Park at the northwest corner of Fifth Avenue and 72nd Street. This walk explores the Conservatory Water and includes surrounding lowlands, pastoral landscapes, some unique fauna, and several treats for children.

The Conservatory Water, known as The Pond in the 1860s, was intended to be the reflecting pool for a large plant conservatory, but because the money could not be appropriated it was never built. In this century the water attracts model boaters, crayfishers, storytellers, jugglers, and visitors who want a brief respite from the crowded city streets. The area is part of a natural depression that lies below street level close to one of the busiest neighborhoods on the Upper East Side.

After the row of benches where two Norway maples form a shady portal, take the path that veers to the right. Behind the pipe rail fence ahead, where the path forks left and right, examine the prickly dark-green needles of the cedars of Lebanon, *Cedrus libani*. This is the northernmost latitude for

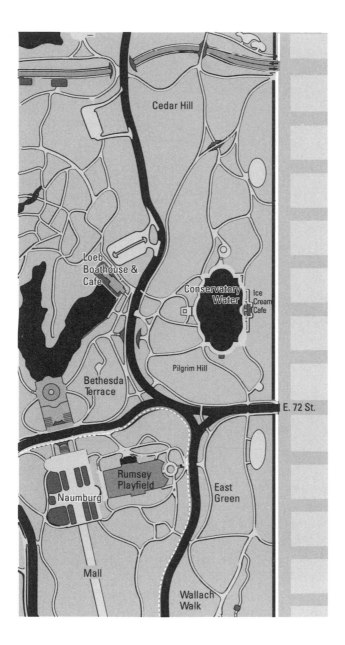

these trees from Asia Minor. Although the trees would be happier in Florida, New York City's microclimate, warmer than outlying areas, allows them to grow successfully here. The cedars are welcome in this landscape for both their beauty and utility. The appeal of their dense blue-green foliage is obvious, but they also protect the vegetation from foot traffic, especially the grassy slope beyond the fence. When mature these cedars can reach heights of one hundred feet or more. Michael Dirr, in his *Manual of Woody Landscape Plants,* champions this cedar as "a specimen tree of unrivaled distinction, uniting the grand with the picturesque." These particular specimens, planted in the 1980s, will need another thirty or forty years of growth before they attain such stature.

Farther along the path to the right, the Waldo Hutchins Memorial Bench honors Waldo Hutchins, president of the Central Park Board of Commissioners from 1889 to 1890. The bench serves as an astronomical calendar on sunny days; the strongly curved design, known architecturally as exedra, allows views of the celestial clock from many points at the base of the bench. The sun's shadow, somewhat obscured by the tree canopy surrounding, casts equinoctial lines indicating the season and time of day.

After the bench, at the first lamppost on the right, an attractive cut-leaf beech, *Fagus sylvatica laciniata,* recognized by its smooth gray bark and tightly serrated leaves, is prominent. These fine trees are cultivated from the European beech. The variety name *laciniata* derives from laciniate, which means slashed into narrow lobes, a reference to the leaves. Seventeen of these beeches are listed throughout the park in the 1982 tree inventory. Another distinguished specimen is encountered at the end of the West Lake Walk. In November, cut-leaf beeches contribute greatly to the park's colorful autumnal foliage, their leaves saturated with bronzes and golds.

The terrain between this path and the wall along Fifth Avenue is planted with trees and shrubs that help screen out the distracting sights and sounds of the avenue. Throughout the park's history dense plantings have been used to screen the perimeter wall. Frederick Law Olmsted foresaw the vastness of the future city as it marched uptown during the nineteenth century. While the park was under construction he wrote:

> The Park will be surrounded by an artificial wall, twice as high as the Great Wall of China, composed of urban buildings. Wherever this should appear across a meadow view, the imagination would be checked abruptly at short range. Natural objects were thus required to be interposed, which, while excluding the buildings as much as possible from view, would leave an uncertainty to the occupation of the space beyond, and establish a horizon line, as much as possible, of verdure.

Olmsted did not foresee the coming of the elevator and the fifty-story high-rises that could not be disguised with verdure; yet the perimeter plantings do create a definite separation between the city and the park.

As the path descends toward the left, a view of the lawn and water unfolds. This path carries us into the pastoral landscape below the level of Fifth Avenue. This dramatic shift away from the cityscape was of prime concern to Olmsted and Vaux. The design intentionally removes park visitors from the rigid and imposing linear grid of streets, replacing them with the picturesque landscape. Once inside the park the topography and plantings suggest a visit to the country. Olmsted appreciated contrasts in the landscape and avoided the predictable. He dictated many general and specific principles on this subject; in the chapter "Plantations," in *Forty Years of*

Landscape Architecture, compiled by his son, Olmsted is specific about these pastoral landscapes:

> To secure interest, it is necessary that some parts of
> the Park should strongly contrast with others. As far
> as space will allow, therefore, smooth, simple, clean
> surfaces of turf on which the light falls early and the
> shadows are broad and trees which have grown freely
> with plenty of room to stretch out their limbs are
> intended to be brought into contrast with surfaces
> which are much broken and on which there is a great
> profusion of lines and colors and lights and shades,
> and with trees and bushes and plants which have
> grown in a somewhat crowded way, bent and mingled
> together as they generally are where native plants
> thrive on rough ground, especially if the soil is rich
> and neither over dry nor over wet.

Many of these shifts from cityscape to pastoral landscape are less dramatic today. Over the years horticulturists and designers have wavered from the pastoral to the formal in landscape design, sometimes incorporating both styles in the same landscape. What distinguishes the Conservatory Water landscape is its power to move us physically and psychologically away from the city. On any given warm, sunny weekend afternoon, the blaring horns and screeching brakes of automobiles on Fifth Avenue above give way to the sounds of soft voices rolling over water and grass.

As you head downhill, look for the blossoms of daffodils, flowering cherries, and crab apples toward the wall in late March and early April. You may also see many migratory birds near the perimeter wall, such as the rufous-sided towhee, the brown thrasher, and numerous species of warblers and sparrows. Few park visitors venture among the thick perimeter plantings, where the ground is strewn with leaf litter and diverse vegetation. Undisturbed ground-feeding birds take advantage of these favorable conditions to search for the insects that are stimulated from dormancy to activity by the warming air.

Across the path from lamppost #7210 a plaque attached to the trunk identifies a Schwedler maple, *Acer platanoides schwedleri,* a variety of the Norway maple. Both Norway and Schwedler maples are recognized by their lightly grooved bark and typically shaped maple leaves. The Schwedler maples differ from Norway maples only by their purple-red color, which is most prominent in spring, before slowly fading to green as chlorophyll increases with the coming of summer.

All photosynthetic plants contain chlorophyll, even when the leaves are red or yellow. Chlorophyll dominates in most photosynthetic plants, such as the Norway maple. However, the red pigment, anthocyanin, has a stronger presence in certain plants, the Schwedler maple among them. This red pigment along with the yellow pigment xanthophyll give the Northeast its spectacular autumnal foliage. As autumn approaches the chlorophyll begins to fade out of the foliage from an effect known as photoperiodism, which occurs when the fading daylight stimulates certain chemical and hormonal responses in plants. Beginning in late September, photoperiodism signals the foliage to cease production of chlorophyll and prepare for dormancy. Yet even as chlorophyll diminishes, photosynthesis continues in the dying leaves. At the advent of frost an abundance of sugar is produced in the leaves as the tree continues to draw nourishment from the ground. The sugar increases the production of red and yellow pigments and in turn gives us our autumnal display.

Continue on to the next juncture of paths, where the sweep of the water and surrounding landscape spreads out to reveal the sunken topography. At this point the park is some one hundred feet below Fifth Avenue. The design of this basin is a well-planned mixture of trees and turf enhanced by the open landscape. Olmsted's son, Frederick Law Olmsted, Jr., wrote about the effect of these pastoral designs in an annotation to his father's writings:

> Finally, there was one simply physical quality that was held of great importance, directly soothing and refreshing to the nerves for reasons we do not understand, at the same time refreshing because of its marked contrast with ordinary urban conditions and because of its pleasant associations. This quality was *verdurousness*—the mere fresh green of vigorous turf and profuse umbrageous foliage.

After lamppost #E–01, take the next path to the right where a Schwedler maple and a stocky red oak mark the entrance to the patio. Up the slope a profusion of white and yellow daffodils spreads across the lawn toward the south wall of the building. Daffodils and other early spring bulbs would seem to be Central Park's favorite flower. Thousands were planted through the 1980s and 1990s, and from mid-March through late April, before many other showy blossoms appear, these flowering bulbs wash over the lawns and roadsides. The common small-cupped daffodil, the large-cupped daffodil, crocus, snowdrops, scilla, and tulips all add to the springtime bloom and offer a welcome change from the winter months of leafless trees. Blossoming immediately after the bulbs are the flowering cherries, which accent the thicket along the wall with puffy pink blossoms in late April through early May. (The park's flowering cherries are discussed on the Reservoir Walk.)

Move on to the flagstone patio, where a plaque above the door of the building reads "Alice H. and Edward A. Kerbs

Memorial," designating this building as the Kerbs Memorial Boathouse. Before the popularity of model boating the Conservatory Water's biggest attraction was ice-skating. A Victorian craze, ice-skating was the first sports activity in the park. At that time a wooden ramp was placed over the steps to prevent damage to the skates and prevent them from chipping the stone. Its popularity lasted until the 1930s, when the water rarely froze sufficiently to skate because New York's winters had become warmer as the city sprawled over Manhattan Island. Another factor preventing freezing was the salt applied to city roads to melt snow, which washed into the park's water bodies through its extensive drainage system. Today NO SKATING signs and ice ladders (should anyone fall through) are placed around all water bodies in the park from December through March. It was not until the 1950s and the construction of Wollman Rink that skating was legally resumed—only it was no longer free.

If it's a hot day, the Ice Cream Cafe offers ice cream and soda as well as tea, coffee, and snacks year-round. This is one of the park's ten stationary food services, including the legendary Tavern on the Green. Another sixty food carts, offering pretzels and hot dogs, are scattered throughout the park.

The northeast corner of the patio at lamppost #7404 is decorated with a Japanese tree lilac, *Syringa japonica amurensis,* a rare find in the park, with fewer than six specimens noted in the 1982 tree inventory. Tree lilacs, small trees reaching only thirty feet, flower in June and attract swarms of bees to their clusters of sweet white blossoms. The common lilac, *Syringa vulgaris,* on the other hand, is a leggy shrub with few lower branches but bushy tops sporting densely clustered purple or white blossoms in late May through mid-June. A magnificent old stand of common lilac is encountered on the Harlem Meer Walk in the Conservatory Garden. The beautiful blossoms of the tree lilac unfortunately emit a somewhat sour fragrance.

For a pleasant odor of lilac we must turn to the common lilac and its fragrance as captured by Walt Whitman: "With many a pointed blossom rising delicate, with the/perfume/strong I love." Although Whitman's line, "a sprig with its flowers I break," in the same poem honors the memory of the recently assassinated Abraham Lincoln, tampering with the vegetation in Central Park, for any reason, breaks the rules and could result in a $100 fine. To enjoy a variety of lilacs and appreciate their diverse blossoms and bloom times, try the Lilac Walk on the northeast edge of Sheep Meadow, located mid-park at 69th Street.

On the northwest corner of the patio, the placement of a European yew, *Taxus spp.,* softens the concrete edge of this structure. Yews are commonly used for this effect in both urban and suburban landscaping. If you look inside the yew you may notice that the branches are covered with bird droppings, euphemistically referred to as whitewash by some birdwatchers. The thick evergreen foliage provides an effective windbreak that helps to protect the birds from the elements and from predators. It's not unusual to see and hear dozens of birds in larger yew hedges and other evergreen shrubs and trees during the winter months. Before guns changed the nature of warfare, the tough wood of the yew was used to manufacture bows. The genus name, *Taxus,* derives from the Greek word for bow. Easy to bend, the yew is the favored wood of Windsor chairs.

At the northeast corner of the water, where the divergent paths are separated by an island of hawthorns, let's stop to search for aquatic wildlife in the four-foot-deep water. The Conservatory Water is more limited in animal and plant species than the other water bodies, in large part because each winter the water in the concrete-lined basin is completely drained and the sediment dredged. Nevertheless, during the spring and summer months some aquatic creatures do

Yew

find their way into the water through the inflow pipe. The clarity of the water, except when there is an algal bloom in late summer, allows close inspection from top to bottom. The 1982 wildlife inventory lists six species of aquatic fauna in the Conservatory Water and the seventh, the crayfish, *Cambarus* sp., is not listed. Those listed are pumpkinseed sunfish, banded killifish, goldfish, crayfish, snails, and a freshwater jellyfish, *Crasoedacusta sowerbyi,* that thrives in aquariums, which in some respects the concrete-lined Conservatory Water resembles.

Waterfowl are much less common on this water body. The lack of vegetative cover discourages birds from settling in, though occasional mallard ducks, gulls, and passing cormorants stop here to feed on the small fish and aquatic insects. If the lack of food and cover were not enough, competition for space from the model boats would certainly discourage the waterfowl from staying. The best waterfowl spotting sites are found on the Lake, Reservoir, and Harlem Meer Walks, where no fewer than forty species of waterfowl and shorebirds can be seen in all four seasons.

Directly north across the path behind the benches, an Asian shrub, the winged euonymous or burning bush, *Euonymous alatus,* proves to be an excellent choice as a barrier planting between the paved paths and the lawn. The "winged" of the common name refers to the small, corky, winglike ridges along the shrub's branches; "burning bush" refers to the shrub's autumn foliage, which is a spectacular fiery display of bursts of deep crimson, rose, and orange. This common landscaping shrub, cryptically named euonymous, or "good name," by Linnaeus, is reported to poison livestock. Poisoned cows notwithstanding, birds eat the seeds without ill effect and many songbirds are sheltered by its dense branches and foliage.

Euonymous lines the path around to the right, almost encircling the *Alice in Wonderland* statue, which is said to have introduced three-dimensional art to countless numbers of children. Designed by José de Creeft in 1960, the eleven-foot-high work portrays Alice seated on a mushroom with the Mad Hatter, the March Hare, the Dormouse, a crocodile, and Alice's kitten, Dinah. Its accessibility offers an opportunity for children to enter its whimsical settings and experience the work directly by sliding over its curves, climbing through its negative spaces, and becoming a chapter of the story.

Rising up by the northeast edge of the statue is a somewhat displaced black willow, *Salix nigra,* recognized by its dark bark and lanceolate leaves. Black willows do best in wetland conditions, yet this specimen, whose tenacious roots have lifted up the concrete and cobblestone, is seemingly out of its habitat. But because it's located in low-lying land where the water table is high, its roots are kept wet. To the left of the willow, behind the railing, a European beech makes a pronounced statement. Even though unusually columnar in form, its smooth, cool gray bark and wavy-edged lanceolate leaves identify it as a beech.

Return to the path around the water and continue along to where the paths diverge in three directions at lamppost #7416. Take a short side tour north by keeping the winged euonymous hedge on the right. Across the path from lamppost

#7516, a group of Austrian pines, *Pinus nigra,* stand on a knoll. The Austrian pines, with 380 specimens listed in the 1982 tree inventory, outnumber all other pines in the park. The next most populous pine is the native white pine, *Pinus strobus,* with 364 specimens. This is the largest single stand of black pines to be found in Central Park. Because their decaying, acidic needles litter the ground, little or nothing grows beneath the pines. Tucked away from the main thoroughfares, their circular placement on this knoll evokes a sense of enchantment. A spiritual sanctuary of sorts, Central Park itself is in large measure a grove of trees in the center of the city. The spirituality of trees has long carried weight and is best examined in Sir James George Frazer's *The Golden Bough.* He surveys the literature and history of the world from Africa to Asia to pre-Columbian America, and to the renowned Druids of the European Celts:

> Amongst the Celts the oak-worship of the Druids is familiar to everyone, and their old word for sanctuary seems to be identical in origin and meaning with the Latin *nemus,* a grove or woodland glade, which still survives in the name of Nemi (a city in Italy and the minor of the moon goddess, Diana).

Visitors with thoughts Druidic often repair to this sanctuary grove of Austrian pines.

Return to lamppost #7416 where the side tour began and continue on to the first set of benches on the right, shaded in summer by a horse chestnut. The many varieties and hybrids of even the most common plants can confuse us with their variable forms. The horse chestnut is no exception. Most encountered in other tours have taller, wider forms, typical of the species. This one's unusual stunted shape adds to the species' diversity. Even without the placard, and despite its atypical form, a close examination of the five-bladed leaf, the dark-gray patchy bark, and unmistakable spiked inflorescence in early May makes identification positive.

Ahead on the right is another literary statue, this time in honor of the Danish storyteller Hans Christian Andersen, which was installed in 1956. Before we consider the statue, take a seat on the bench at lamppost #7420 to hear the saga of the two red-tailed hawks, *Buteo jamaicensis,* who successfully mated, nested, and gave birth to a brood of three chicks nearby in 1995. Unsuccessful in 1993 and again in 1994, the hawks chose their nesting sites from among the buildings on Fifth Avenue. The first attempts produced eggs that hatched nothing but frustration, especially for the park's bird-watching community, which stood daily vigil below the nests, observing with binoculars and pacing to and fro below like hopeful, expectant parents.

In the spring of 1995, the hawks built a nest on the top ledge of the topmost window of the shorter building seen across the water a bit to the right of the Ice Cream Cafe. The event attracted bird-watchers and journalists nationwide. In his 1964 book, *Birds of the New York Area,* John Bull states, "The red-tailed hawk has decreased considerably in the past thirty years or so. It breeds in the wilder sections of the interior highlands and in pine and oak barrens of eastern Long Island." These beautiful, at-risk raptors, which breed in wildlands, were seen nesting in the middle of Manhattan. Of course such a story would attract attention.

During the weeks the hawks built the nest and laid and incubated the eggs, each development was tracked in local newspapers. The event offered the experience of witnessing a prodigious natural event in the most urban setting imaginable, while extending an opportunity to unify strangers who watched the hawks. At one point the owners of the apartment of the nest building on Fifth Avenue invited the bird-watchers up for closer observation.

After the hawk chicks hatched, the word spread through the park, eventually reaching the desk of the Parks Department's Maintenance and Operations facility. Concern for the hawk chicks ran deep. Their preferred food, rodents, which include rats and squirrels, was abundant in the park. But the Parks Department's rat-baiting policy troubled the hawk-watchers. Not enough information was available about the rodenticides to assuage their fears that rats who had eaten the poison might poison the hawk chicks in turn. The Parks Department was reluctant to change its rat-baiting policy, concerned that public opinion would prevent them from baiting again after the chicks had grown and the rats multiplied to epidemic numbers.

But an event as dynamic as hawks being born in Central Park transcends even the bureaucracy of urban politics. Because all the concerned parties possessed an acute awareness of the environmental and ecological significance of the hawks and their chicks in an urban park, the Parks Department agreed to suspend rat baiting.

Through the spring and well into early summer, as the parent hawks taught the fledglings to hunt, but continued to feed them, the rats, although safe from poisoning, were under constant threat from the raptors. Later that summer the fledglings were observed hunting for themselves. The most frequented hunting areas were noted and rat baiting was excluded from the hunting areas. When the chicks were fending for themselves and the rats began to multiply, baiting continued on a regular basis with no apparent harm to the hawks. By summer's end the young hawks left the park for territories of their own. The story had a truly happy ending when, in the spring of 1996, the parents successfully nested again, on the same window ledge, and hatched three more chicks.

On summer weekends storytellers and clowns entertain at the Hans Christian Andersen statue. The work was sculpted by George Lober and installed on this spot in 1956. As with

Alice in Wonderland, it represents Central Park's longstanding commitment to children, which began when Olmsted and Vaux created the children's district south of the 65th Street Transverse Road. The Dairy, originally designed to distribute milk and snacks to children when the park opened, was followed by the carousel in 1872. Whirling to an old-fashioned calliope, the carousel features magnificent hand-carved horses. Nearby is the Kinderberg Arbor, a 110-foot, circular rustic shelter, constructed on Children's Mountain, now the site of the Chess and Checkers House. Today many park attractions focus on children and include the educational facilities at Dana Center and Belvedere Castle; the Swedish Cottage marionette theater; the Children's Zoo; North Meadow Recreation Center; and twenty playgrounds with various features such as wading pools, slides, and climbing apparatus. When stories are not being told at the Hans Christian Andersen statue, children can still enjoy the sculpture by climbing and reclining on Hans's lap or by considering the ugly duckling and Andersen's moral of the tale: "It matters little to be born in a duck-yard when one comes from a swan's egg."

A variety of shrubs and ground cover neatly frames the space immediately behind the statue. The Japanese andromeda, *Pieris japonica,* a leggy shrub recognized by its evergreen foliage, displays clusters of white bell-shaped flowers in mid-April through much of May. In late April through mid-May the shade-tolerant American redbud, *Cercis canadensis,* is easily recognized by the streams of red-lavender flowers covering the branches before the foliage appears in the form of large, four-to-six-inch rounded to heart-shaped leaves on spindly stems. Mature redbuds have smooth dark bark with fine gray grooves. Because of their showy flowers they are often used as native landscaping trees. In their natural habitat—the moist, rich woods of the Appalachian Cove forests of Tennessee and Kentucky—they grow as understory trees, much as the flowering dogwood does here. Although hardwood trees, the red-buds in Central Park must be planted away from paths or playgrounds, where their thin branches are easily broken. Beyond the slope from the andromeda and redbud more daf-fodils blanket the turf, displaying yellow and white flowers like a multitude of smiling faces from late March through mid-April. Beyond the daffodils, toward the East Drive, the pink and white blossoms of the flowering Kwanzan cherries attract our attention in early spring.

Redbud

Back at the water, another path diverges off to the right between two London plane trees. A few feet up the path on the left a Korean dogwood, *Cornus mas,* will be in full yellow flower at the end of March before its leaves appear. As with the redbud and several other trees and shrubs, this dogwood depends upon cool weather insects for pollination and extends its floral fanfare before many other trees and shrubs have begun leafing out or flowering. The bumblebees, family *Bombidae,* do most of the pollinating of these early flowering species in the morning. The bumblebee's "sweater," the dense hair covering its body, protects it from the cold and gives it an advantage in collecting the morning's first nectar while other insects remain torpid before being warmed and stimulated by the sun.

Before the next concession stand, a path swings around and up the hill. Three stately pin oaks, majestic testaments to their species and likely candidates for original park plantings, stand at the corner of the path. The crowns of the pin oaks lean slightly away from each other, so we may assume that they were all planted at the same time. As the trees grew their crowns positioned themselves for maximum exposure to the sun. The younger London plane trees to the right seem to be an afterthought in the planting design of this landscape, their thickness inappropriate to the columnar grandeur of the statuesque oaks.

Past lamppost #7216, up the hill on the right, an infrequently occurring native tree in the park, the scarlet oak, *Quercus coccinea,* rises up from the compacted soil. The 1982 inventory lists only twenty scarlet oaks. They closely resemble the pin oaks and are best distinguished by their acorn cups, which are larger and deeper than the pin oaks'. In their natural environment the two oaks are more easily distinguished, as the pin oak grows in moister bottomlands, while the scarlet oak prefers drier uplands. In Central Park, where the pin oak is the third most common tree, growing equally in uplands and bottomlands, this environmental distinction does not apply.

At the top of the first set of stairs, on the right, a small Ohio buckeye, *Aesculus glabra,* a native tree found commonly farther west and south of New York, reaches over the thorny barberry shrubs toward the path. When mature this tree will dominate the steps and cast a welcome cooling shade. (An original park planting of an Ohio buckeye is examined on the 100th Street Pool Walk.)

The walk ends where it began, at the second set of stairs ahead by the Lebanon cedars and exedra bench. Henry James, the novelist and starchy social critic, upon returning to the United States from his self-imposed exile in England, still found much to criticize about his homeland in his 1905 book,

The American Scene, but of Central Park he could impart only praise:

> The condensed geographical range, the number of kinds of scenery in a given space, competed with the number of languages heard, and the whole impression was of one's having had but to turn in from the Plaza to make, in the most agreeable manner possible, the tour of the little globe. And that, frankly, I think, was the best of all impressions—was seeing New York at its best; for if one could feel at one's best about the "social question," it would be surely, somehow, on such an occasion.

Long-eared Owl

59th Street Pond Walk

The Pond,
Central Park South and Avenue of the Americas

THIS WALK CIRCUMNAVIGATES the 59th Street Pond, a remnant of the pre-park waterway known in the nineteenth century as DeVoor's Mill Stream. Along the way we'll explore three statues, two bridges, the Cop Cot rustic shelter, and the Hallett Nature Sanctuary.

Begin this tour at the statue of José Martí, located at the Avenue of the Americas (Sixth Avenue) and Central Park South. Martí was a Cuban poet and national hero of Cuba's struggle for independence from Spain. He died in battle in 1895. The statue, sculpted by Anna Hyatt Huntingdon and presented to the park in 1965, is one of only a few works in the park that commemorate national heroes after World War I—a barbarous war that unsettled America's ideas about heroism and therefore produced few individual war heroes. The only monument dedicated to World War I is Karl M. Illava's *Seventh Regiment* at Fifth Avenue and 67th Street; erected ten years after the war, it honors the common soldier. Most of the statuary after 1918 is whimsical, as observed in the various

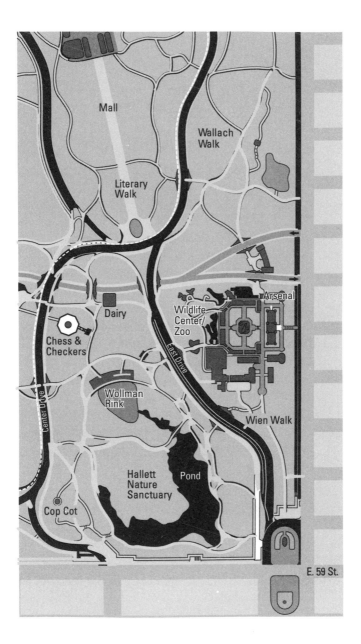

Mall

Wallach
Walk

Literary
Walk

Dairy

Chess &
Checkers

Wildlife
Center/
Zoo

Arsenal

Center Drive

East Drive

Wollman
Rink

Wien Walk

Hallett
Nature
Sanctuary

Pond

Cop Cot

E. 59 St.

animal and literary sculptures such as *Alice in Wonderland* and Hans Christian Andersen on the Conservatory Water Walk. The last piece of sculpture placed in the park, in 1991, is a bronze cast of Paul Manship's *Group of Bears,* located in the playground just south of the Metropolitan Museum of Art at 79th Street.

A set of stairs descends into the park to the left of the Martí statue. Note the vegetation on the slope on the right. This commonly used spreading euonymous, *Euonymous fortunei,* stabilizes the soil and protects it against erosion. During heavy rains its dense, evergreen foliage deflects the drops that would otherwise erode the soil from the slope, while its roots hold the soil in place. Where it's not trampled, spreading euonymous becomes dense, as seen here, and will climb trees and fences. Where foot traffic is heavy the ground cover requires periodic replacement.

As a whole, the plants that surround the Pond are not consistent with any particular school of landscape design. Throughout the past century, many designers and horticulturists have applied various planting schemes to this location. In the late nineteenth century the Pond was planted with bald cypress, golden rain tree, an abundance of speckled alder, willow, Spanish chestnut, balsam fir, guelder-rose (*Viburnum opulus*), and a smattering of mountain laurel, paper mulberry, euonymous, and scores of wildflowers. Today a more limited variety of vegetation ornaments the Pond, including a stand of weeping spruces, several varieties of hawthorn, scattered witch hazels, and a speckling of wildflowers.

The first tree near the path after the first lamppost, #5928, is a young Chinese scholar tree, *Sophora japonica,* no more than forty years old. It can be recognized by its six-to-ten-inch fernlike leaves and lightly furrowed dark brown bark. At first glance, the young scholar tree can be mistaken for its relatives the honey locust and the black locust. Farther along on the walk, a honey locust and a black locust will be compared.

Scholar trees tolerate harsh urban conditions, making them good park and street trees. They are attractive in all seasons, displaying their foot-long, fragrant, cream-colored clusters of flowers in late summer that become decorative yellowish fruit pods lasting well into winter. Across the path, three more scholar trees, about the same age, descend the hill toward the water. Larger, statuesque specimens of the scholar tree are encountered on the West Lake Walk.

At the foot of the stairs, take a moment to marvel at the topography surrounding the Pond and the mountainous sky-line of Fifth Avenue and Central Park South (59th Street) beyond. The landscape surrounding the Pond was fashioned from DeVoor's Mill Stream, a shallow rivulet surrounded by a swamp, which ran from this area to the East River (today the average depth of the 3.5-acre Pond is 2½ feet). The water from the Pond now flows to the Newtown Creek Treatment Plant in Brooklyn, where it is filtered and returned to the East River.

During construction of the park only minor changes in topography occurred around the Pond. In the nineteenth century, DeVoor's Mill Stream ran through this shallow depression in the landscape at the same level that it flows today. The most radical alteration to this landscape was the raising of the slope up to 59th Street in order to further remove the city from the park. In their original design, Frederick Olmsted and Calvert Vaux envisioned the Pond this way:

> [It] is proposed to form a lake of irregular shape, and with an area of eight or nine acres. . . . It is conceived that, by introducing such an ornamental sheet of water into the composition at this point, the pic-turesque effect of the bold bluffs that will run down to its edge and overhang it, must be much increased; and that by means of such a natural boundary, this rocky section of the Park will be rendered more retired and attractive as a pleasant walk or lounge.

In the 1860s, the entrance to the park from Fifth Avenue and 59th Street was the most popular (the Sixth and Seventh Avenue entrances at 59th Street were added later) and the Pond was often the first landscape seen by visitors. Once on the path around the Pond, visitors were shielded from the city by a green wall of trees and shrubs. The skyline of today, with its tall, looming buildings, did not exist then, and the sounds of traffic beyond the wall—mostly from horse-drawn carriages—could probably not be heard at this low elevation, a mere twenty feet above sea level. Even today, the honking and revved-up automobile and truck noises are a distant drone, easily ignored in this setting.

From the bottom of the stairs follow the path to the right. Behind the first set of benches, viburnum and euonymous shrubs surround a willow oak, *Quercus phellos*. Over a hundred willow oaks were counted in the 1982 tree survey. Note the narrow, willowlike, lance-shaped leaves, peculiar to these oaks. Willow oaks naturally occur farther south, from New Jersey to Florida; however, their abundance in New York greatly increased after the designers of Central Park made them a popular urban park planting, discovering the trees' attractive form and grace.

Farther ahead, along the edge of the wall that separates the path from the slope to 59th Street, an assortment of weeds and wildflowers take advantage of the light, the warm rocks, and the rich silt deposited by erosion from up the slope. Some of the common species here, also found scattered throughout the park, include: galinsoga, *G. cilita,* nearly identical to wild quinine but with smaller flowers one-quarter inch across with five tiny white petals blooming through most of the summer; daisy fleabane, *Erigeron annus,* an attractive asterlike flower, one-to-three-feet tall with fifty or so white to magenta-colored rays on each tiny blossom in midsummer; yellow wood sorrel, *Oxalis stricta,* a three-to-four-inch plant easily mistaken for clover because of its three leaves, but with distinctive small yellow flowers in early and midsummer; snakeroot, *Eupatorium rugosum,* three feet tall with flat-top clusters of small, fuzzy white flowers from September to November, with leaf and stem structure similar to white wood aster but with opposite leaves; common nightshade, *Solanum nigrum,* its small flowers with five reflexed white petals and tiny yellow beak formed by the stamens in early to midsummer, becoming small clusters of inedible black fruit in autumn; green amaranth, also known as Mexican tea, *Amaranthus retroflexus,* which can grow to six feet, with dense spikes of weedy-looking, chaffy, greenish flowers in late summer. Also, in March and April a profusion of daffodils speckle portions of this slope; these are especially attractive when they float up through the viney ground cover.

At the next unnumbered lamppost, locate the cedar of Lebanon, *Cedrus lebani,* which we encountered in a dense group on the Conservatory Water Walk. This cedar is recognized by bluish green needles and light-brown scaly bark, and by its bulbous, light-green cones growing from branches in late June through August. This cedar is wrongly placed on this spot, however. In order to attain the sweeping stature for which the cedar of Lebanon is recognized worldwide, it requires more sunlight and richer soil. One can only guess at the intentions of the designer or plantsman who put it here. Nonetheless, whether you enjoy it for its rarity or its beauty, it is a pleasant discovery.

About thirty feet down the path from the unnumbered lamppost, a medium-size, thornless honey locust, *Gleditsia triacanthos var. inermis,* is recognized by its lightly flaked, gray-brown bark with greenish tinge. Horticulturists of the early twentieth century collected seeds from the thornless specimens of honey locusts in the wild and propagated them for use in public areas. A thorny honey locust is examined on the Turtle Pond Walk. Other than the thorns, the trees are identical.

At the next lamppost, also unnumbered, look to the right for the double-file viburnum, *Viburnum tomentosum,* one of the most common shrubs in the park. This viburnum can be recognized by its distinctively crinkled, broad opposite leaves and attractive snowy-white, saucerlike flowerheads in mid-May that are arranged in double file along the arching branches. Small reddish, egg-shaped, berrylike fruits replace the flowers in July and August. Another Chinese scholar tree, its branches growing over and into the lamppost immediately behind the double-file viburnum, allows us to compare its leaf and bark to the honey locust at the previous lamppost.

From lamppost #N224 at the end of the row of benches, take a moment to reexamine the skyline of Fifth Avenue. More of its buildings have become evident as the landscape sweeps toward the east. A vista from this arm of the Pond sweeps over the water to the turf beyond, then rises subtly skyward to connect with Fifth Avenue behind the trees. The view suits Olmsted and Vaux's vision of the broad yet simple pastoral landscape. Olmsted wrote specifically to the gardeners of the nineteenth century on the subject of pastoral landscapes:

> The special value of the Central Park will lie in its comparative largeness. There are certain kinds of beauty possible. Such beauty as there is in a flower bed, such beauty as there is in a fir tree or a cluster of trees can be enjoyed on any piece of flat ground of a quarter of an acre, can be had even in the back yard of a city house. The seven hundred acres of the Central Park can be better used. That which is expected to be especially valuable on the Central Park is the beauty of broad landscape scenes and of combinations of trees with rocks and turf and water.

Across from lamppost #5916, a stand of the evergreen shrub inkberry, *Ilex glabra compacta,* has grown high enough to block the view to the water. This cultivar, "compacta," a hybrid of the wild species, remains tightly foliated. In the wild, inkberry is found commonly in wetlands, but its open, leggy appearance makes it unsuitable for most parks and gardens. Being fairly tolerant of urban conditions, it is found in many parks and formal landscape designs. This hedge was not intended to block the view of the water but rather to be viewed from the other side of the Pond, where its dense foliage composes an admirable element in the landscape that combines with the twisted shape of the leafless crab apple and the evergreen yew, to be visited shortly.

The reeds covering much of the Pond's shoreline are phragmites, *Phragmite communis*. Many plant ecologists have dubbed phragmite "the scourge of the wetland" because it is one of the most pernicious weeds to invade our shores from Europe. A society of restoration ecologists, naturalists, and champions of native plants have dedicated themselves to the eradication of this plant. Phragmites aggressively displace native vegetation and form pure stands that cause serious ecological imbalances in wetland areas. This in turn interferes with the quality, filtration, and flow of the groundwater that ultimately becomes our drinking water. However, phragmite is only one of several aggressive alien species that upset the balance of our local ecosystems. Awareness of this problem has prompted a movement to promote the use of more native plant species in landscape designs and soil reclamation projects. Even Olmsted, writing in his later years, with greater insight into the landscape experience, advocated the use of more native and fewer alien gardenesque species:

> Plants indigenous to the park and vicinity should predominate in the planting, and should be planted into conditions similar to those in which they are growing wild. Garden forms and exotic plants should as a rule not be used in any part of the park with the exception

of the following kinds, which are either natives of other parts of the country, similar to natives in character, or especially adapted to certain conditions.

On the left between the water fountain and the fire hydrant, a small stand of yew, *Taxus* sp., is recognized by its soft evergreen needles. Yews make perfect low hedges because their dense habit and full texture work both as a barrier plant and as a year-round embellishment to most landscapes. Although some sources claim the yew to be toxic to humans, the berries are eaten by many birds. In the wild, deer and moose eat the foliage.

The young tree near the edge of the water growing from the yew hedge is a perfectly placed sour gum, *Nyssa sylvatica,* a lover of wet landscapes described on the West Lake Walk. This specimen, less than six inches in diameter in 1982, wasn't included with the twenty-seven tupelos counted in the 1982 tree inventory. Notice that the branches on the water side of the tree are fuller and longer than those in the shade and that the trunk leans slightly toward the light over the open water. Many contemporary plantsmen, following the dictates of the natural world, plant trees with a compensated lean toward the light. In forest openings, along streams, lakes, meadows, and even along roadways, trees naturally lean toward the sunlight. Planting trees straight up and down along these natural edges often results in curved tree trunks and an unnatural appearance to the landscape as a whole.

Continue along until the path veers sharply to the left at lamppost #5912. A section of the N and R–line subway appears through the open grates in the park wall along 59th Street. The subway has caused some serious problems for the trees along the sidewalk above it. Where most street tree pits are four-by-four-foot openings that allow water and aeration to the trees' roots, the tree pits above the subway have been cemented in to prevent water from entering the tracks. Ironically, while most street trees have difficulty finding enough water in the harsh urban substrate the trees over the 59th Street subway are slowly drowning. To date no solutions to this dilemma have surfaced.

Step up to the pipe rail on the edge of the water along the path to your left. The outflow pipe for the Pond can be seen at the water's edge. From there the water is carried to the Newtown Creek treatment plant.

From the pipe rail a broad, pastoral view extends over the water to the ivy-covered Gapstow Bridge on the far side of the Pond. The original Gapstow Bridge, completed in 1874, was unique in using cast iron and wood for construction. However, wear and tear took its toll on the structure and before the turn of the century it had to be rebuilt. The present bridge, designed and completed in 1896, is constructed of unadorned Manhattan schist (the bedrock of Manhattan Island), which makes the bridge sturdier. We'll discuss this bridge more fully when we come to it.

For now, consider the landscape textures of the opposing banks. To the left, on the western bank, phragmites dominate the shoreline. Yet even though invasive along the water's edge they seem somehow fitting among that shore's verdure, completing the transition from dense woodland to open water—although this is no testament for phragmites in the Park. Most of the wildlife around the Pond occurs along the western shore (the water edge of Hallett Sanctuary, discussed later on the tour). Egrets and herons commonly hunt for fish along that edge and mallard ducks often nest there. By contrast, the stone and mortar bank of the eastern shoreline has no inviting edge to support wildlife. It is the west bank's rough texture that attracts the animals, and it is so rustic by comparison that even the pigeons flying over the water seem less an urban nuisance than pleasant additions to the scenic landscape.

Return to lamppost #5912 on the path that parallels 59th Street and continue on through the stand of English elms and ginkgoes that line the walkway. A stairway exits the park where the path curves around to the left. This tour will follow the path to the left, but first a side tour out of the park briefly explores Grand Army Plaza at the corners of Fifth Avenue and 59th and 60th Streets. If it's a hot sunny afternoon, your first sensory experience will be the odor of horses from the hansom carriages that congregate here and along 59th Street waiting for tourists to experience the thrill of those famous words, "Once around the park," at a cost of $35 a half hour.

Cross the street to the oval plaza where the equestrian statue of William Tecumseh Sherman shines in its recent application of gold leaf and struts its rugged, heroic form. After Ulysses S. Grant, Sherman was the second most important Union general of the Civil War. The statue, commissioned to the renowned sculptor Augustus Saint-Gaudens in 1892, was modeled from life by Saint-Gaudens as Sherman sat two hours a week for the artist. The work is considered by many critics to be one of the preeminent equestrian statues in America. Begun in 1892, it was completed in 1897 and won a Grand Prix at the Paris Exposition in 1900. After a bit of haggling over where to install the statue in New York—the Grant family didn't want it in front of Grant's Tomb—it was ceremoniously unveiled here in 1903.

Grand Army Plaza, half the size at the time, had to be enlarged to accommodate the enormous monument. Today the plaza is heavily planted with colorful bulbs and annuals donated by occupants of the buildings on Fifth Avenue and planted by the Central Park Conservancy. Bradford Callery pears, *Pyrus calleryana,* line the northern edge of the plaza, and in early spring it shimmers with magnificent white blossoms. These non-fruiting pear trees are among the most urban tolerant and therefore most widely planted street trees in New York City.

After exploring Grand Army Plaza, return to the park and continue along the path on the right. Stop at the European beech, *Fagus sylvatica,* the first tree on the left after the paths diverge. This beech is recognized not only by the typically smooth gray bark of all beeches but also by the graffiti etched into it. Beeches, because of their smooth, soft bark, commonly attract graffiti vandals much the way mud puddles attract splashing children. Fortunately, the graffiti is usually less damaging than the lack of respect the vandals have for the tree. All trees possess complex defense mechanisms that protect their inner structures from chance injury, such as graffiti or storm damage. One of a tree's most important components, the vascular system (a single-celled layer located just beneath the bark), conducts nutrients between roots and leaves. In thin-barked trees like beeches the vascular system is only a fraction of an inch below the bark. When damaged, the system emits chemicals that harden off the wound and form a scarlike closure. This is not tacit encouragement for graffiti, but it is reassuring to know that trees are not without defenses.

At the connection of paths ahead a large rock outcrop, surrounded by forsythia and barberry, rises up from the edge of the water. To the right of the outcrop a perfectly shaped American elm, *Ulmus americana,* shades the rock. Mature elms normally attain heights from sixty to eighty feet and more, but this elm's stunted size—because of its location on the outcrop—allows us to see its splendidly well-formed and classically vase-shaped crown. Along Fifth Avenue, where the largest contiguous stand of American elms exist on the continent, many more mature, magnificent elm specimens tower over the park.

Where the paths diverge up ahead at lamppost #6016 take a moment to turn around and admire the prominent Manhattan skyline, composed here from east to west of the buildings between the Plaza Hotel and the Essex House on Central Park South. This view would certainly have repulsed Olmsted and

Vaux, who took great pains to screen out the city's abutment against the park with tall shrubs and trees.

As mentioned, the park's edge along 59th Street was deliberately made steep and planted with tall trees to remove the view of the city along that path. Nearly three hundred white ash, whose height and bushy crowns easily disguised the four- and five-story buildings of the mid-1800s, were planted atop the high ridge. Visitors entering the park from the Fifth Avenue entrance literally left the city behind them.

Ironically, and it is irony of the highest sense, the beginning of the park's construction in 1857 was the year that Elisha Groves Otis demonstrated his new invention, the elevator. A few years later Manhattan's rising skyline was well under way and trees could no longer disguise the buildings. The loftiest trees on earth (the Founder's Tree, a coastal redwood in California's Humboldt National State Park, is the record holder) reach heights of three hundred feet, or approximately thirty stories. By 1900, city buildings exceeded forty stories. Today there are very few locations in the park where buildings cannot be seen (the best is found around the Loch, where at any given spot no trace of the city is visible). And yet, though most parkscapes are more pleasurable without a view of the city, there is a certain monumental appeal to the textures and hues of the skyscrapers towering over the park, adding yet another dimension to our living work of art—here the city is held at bay by the walls of this fragile yet enduring Central Park.

From lamppost #6016, we'll follow the path left along the water's edge, but first a detour to the right takes us to the bust of Thomas Moore. The statue was donated by the Friendly Sons of St. Patrick Society in 1880 to commemorate the popular Irish poet's centennial birthday. Moore wrote a series of poems entitled *Irish Melodies,* one of the most popular being "The Last Rose of Summer." Among his other works are biographies of the British poet Lord Byron and the Irish dramatist Richard Brinsley Sheridan. The larger-than-life bronze bust is by Dennis B. Sheahan, an Irish sculptor.

Return to the path where you departed from it for the Moore statue and head left along the water to the first intersection, which veers sharply right at the end of the benches. Examine the three large rocks at the intersection. In the center rock look for the three-inch hole drilled into it. Holes like these were made by nineteenth-century stonecutters using hand drills to split large rocks and boulders. Into the holes they inserted beveled rods called feather wedges and then wedged a larger iron rod between them. The rod was hammered between the wedges until the rock split. The pieces were fitted into bridges and other structures where stone was needed for support. Many of the park's arches and foundations were fitted with stones and boulders excavated during its more than ten years of construction, when more than ten million wagonloads of rock and soil were moved in and out of the park. When completed in 1873, the park was tidied up and materials not used for structural support, such as these rocks, were used as edging and accents in the landscape.

A dense planting of shrubs lines the path on the right. The dominant plants are a variety of the genus *Cotoneaster,* members of the rose family and closely related to hawthorn. The cotoneasters' low, dense habit and small, mostly evergreen foliage help to identify them. This thicket, even though continually surrounded by human activity, attracts a flurry of bird activity. The dense shrubs prevent trampling between the upper and lower paths while offering safe habitat and nesting potential for several common urban birds such as grackles, sparrows, and starlings. The fruits of the cotoneaster and other shrubs here quickly disappear after the birds discover them.

Nearly forty species of birds have been known to nest in Central Park throughout its history. Only about half that many nest regularly today because of habitat loss and increased human disturbance. As early as 1886, L. B. Woodruff and A. G. Paine in "Birds of Central Park" in the magazine *Forest and Stream* documented seventy-two species including quail, bluebirds, meadowlark, warblers, and others that no longer reside and some which no longer even visit. Since then a number of such compilations of bird populations have appeared, the most recent being an annotated checklist compiled by the Birdwatchers of Central Park and published by the Central Park Conservancy in 1995.

The path divides ahead. We'll follow it up the stairs to the right and to the next intersection to examine Inscope Arch under the East Drive. This bridge, another Calvert Vaux design, was constructed in 1875, two years after the park was officially completed. Inscope's construction was precipitated by public outcry over the bottleneck of pedestrians crossing the drive on the way to the Zoo (unofficially the oldest in the country), which conflicted with the carriages driving into the park from the south. The arch channeled and dispersed some of that pedestrian traffic. The beautiful Inscope Arch, constructed from pink and white granite, is twelve feet high and thirty-four feet long. It was built over the remains of the same swamp through which DeVoor's Mill Stream flowed and from which the 59th Street Pond was fashioned. Unfortunately, after draining the water for the Pond, a quagmire remained around the bridge location and extra timber and brick had to be installed for the support and construction of Inscope. This caused project costs to mount to $50,000, considerably higher than the other arches and bridges in the park. Over a hundred years later, in 1983, Inscope was cleaned and painted and its interior lighting repaired to make it a safe and pleasant scenic route to the Zoo.

Return to the path paralleling the water. At lamppost #6220 the path diverges in five directions. We'll follow the second path on the left, leading to Gapstow Bridge. On the left of the path, a new tree to these tours, the common catalpa, *Catalpa bignonioides,* can be recognized by the scaly, light-brown trunk and very large heart-shaped leaves. *The 1982 Tree Inventory* lists 53 catalpas parkwide. Through most of the year their long fruit pods, like attenuated cigars, are visible to help with identification. In mid-June their tubular, spectacularly showy white blossoms with purple and yellow blotches appear on the tree. The flowers are not always visible in the heights of the tree, but after fertilization by bees and other insects they are released from the branches and can be found decorating the ground. The catalpa is another southerly tree, like the Osage orange and willow oak, introduced to the Northeast over the past hundred years. It now grows as far north as the Catskill Mountains. In their native region of Tennessee and Arkansas, catalpas grow near streams and in wet woods, but they will tolerate many growing conditions. The tree's formidably syllabled species name, *bignonioides,* honors Jean-Paul Bignon, a court librarian in Paris who died in 1743 and who was respected by Thomas Walter, the taxonomist who named the species.

Catalpa

Facing south from the deck of Gapstow Bridge, another monumental view of 59th Street spreads out beyond the Pond and over the trees toward the Plaza Hotel. But looking north we face a deflated view of the landscape and Wollman Rink, with its inappropriate midcentury architecture in an otherwise Victorian design. Wollman Rink, built in 1951 during the recreation-minded Robert Moses's tenure as Parks Commissioner, reduced the size of the Pond from five to three acres. There was much public outcry over construction of the rink, as there has always been over any usurpation of acreage from the Central Park landscape. Nonetheless, Wollman Rink attracts crowds in all seasons.

Jacob Wrey Mould designed the original Gapstow Bridge, as well as many of the park's structures, including the splendid Moorish designs and ornamentation of Bethesda Terrace, visited on the East Lake Walk. The stone arch design of Gapstow unfortunately no longer bears the ornate style of Mould. The original bridge, built in 1874, featured wood planking and stone abutments, together with an arched cast-iron railing and an ornate motif of smaller decorative arches, each centered with three cinquefoils. By 1896, the bridge was redesigned and rebuilt with tough Manhattan schist into this simpler but sturdier structure. The current bridge spans seventy-six feet with a twelve-foot-high arch.

Leaving Gapstow we also leave the Pond, and edge along the chain-link fence surrounding Hallett Nature Sanctuary, named in honor of George Hervey Hallett, Jr., a New York nature lover. The sanctuary, called The Promontory in the nineteenth century because its rock outcrop projects into the Pond, is now more commonly called the Bird Sanctuary. Although some birds do frequent the area on the edges of the water, there are fewer birds found here than in the Ramble or North Woods. Two factors attribute to this: cats and automobiles. The Bird Sanctuary, closed to the public, frequently becomes home to feral cats who prey on the birds for food. Also, the area's proximity to noisy 59th Street dissuades interior-dwelling forest birds, such as the deep-woods war-blers, from frequenting the environment.

At the end of the chain-link fence, take the second path that bears left. An unnumbered lamppost sprouts out of a yew hedge at the corner of the path. The path inclines through a portal of two black locusts to another juncture of paths at the base of a large rock outcrop.

Leave the path across from lamppost #6030 and venture up the long, smooth outcrop to the rustic shelter atop the grassy knoll. The grooved indentures of the outcrop were carved by the Wisconsin glacier fifteen thousand years ago. The alternating light and dark parallel bands, known as folia-tions, running north and south along the outcrop, were exposed as the glacier scored the rock. The lighter, cream-colored bands are composed of quartz and feldspar and are raised slightly above the darker ones, which are composed of mica and hornblende. Because the quartz and feldspar were more durable than the mica and hornblende, they wore down more slowly. Over the thousands of years since the glacier carved the groove into this outcrop the rain and wind have weathered the rocks and created the raised ridges.

At the top of the rock outcrop, a narrow cinder path curves slightly to the rustic shelter at the apex of the knoll. This shelter was named Cop Cot by Olmsted from a combination of Old English words meaning little house (or *cot*tage) on the crest of a hill (cop). Fifteen of these rustic shelters, then called summer-houses, adorned the park in the nineteenth century but were removed as they fell into disrepair. Two of the summerhouses, this one and another visited on the West Lake Walk in the Ram-ble, were rebuilt in the 1980s by the restoration crew of the Central Park Conservancy in the same style and from the same type of wood, unhewn cedar, used in the original design.

Surrounding the summerhouse a number of white pines, hemlock, and an English holly give the area a sense of the rural. In cold weather the evergreen English holly becomes a shelter to dozens of English sparrows whose chattering and scurrying about contributes to the overall sense of the Cop Cot's country atmosphere.

At this elevation, about eighty feet above the park, a commanding view of the surrounding parkscape and the tops of some of the trees can be enjoyed. On the southwest edge of the outcrop a mature red maple, *Acer rubrum,* twists up from a rocky knoll below. A precarious examination of the maple's buds, flowers, and leaves can be obtained from the edge, but proceed cautiously as the rocks may be slippery.

Yucca

The walk ends here in the restful setting of the summerhouse. To return to 59th Street where the walk began follow the path that winds down the south side of the outcrop past tastefully placed beds of euonymous and a rare plant in the park, yucca, *Yucca filamentosa,* known and recognized by its other common name, Spanish bayonet, which describes the long, spiked leaves radiating up from its basal clump. Yucca works well here because of the sparse ground cover under tall trees on a barren rock outcrop. A cluster of bell-shaped, whitish green flowers rises up on a woody stalk from the center of the yucca leaves in late summer.

Appendix A

Other Points of Interest

The Dairy (mid-park at 65th Street): Milk was distributed here in early park days, when the south end of the park below the 65th Street Transverse Road was known as the Children's District. Since the 1980s the Dairy has served as a visitor's center offering directions, maps, and historical information.

Chess and Checkers House (nearby and west of the Dairy): Originally the site of the Kinderborg Arbor, this is the park's largest rustic structure at 110 feet across, built atop a rock outcrop known as Children's Mountain. An enclosed octagonal structure used for educational programs now occupies the site. Permanent checkerboard tables are available outside the house.

Sheep Meadow (between 66th and 69th Streets off West Drive): Originally a military parade ground, now the largest "quiet zone" in Central Park awash with sunbathers and the scent of coconut oil on sunny summer weekends. Sports and dogs are prohibited, and the panoramic views of Manhattan spectacular. Sheep once grazed here to add picturesqueness to the park.

The Mall (stretching from 66th to 72nd Streets mid-park): Although mentioned in the walks, a visit to Central Park would be incomplete without a visit to the Mall. Famous for its grand formality, found nowhere else in the park, it features ancient elms, classic statuary, the largest tree in the park, the first piece of sculpture (von Schiller, moved from the Ramble), and the incomparable design and carvings of Bethesda Terrace, briefly described on the East Lake Walk.

Strawberry Fields (71st to 73rd Streets west of West Drive): An impeccably tended homage to John Lennon donated by Yoko Ono featuring a tile mosaic imprinted with "IMAGINE," the title of one of Lennon's most memorable songs. The landscape attracts many peaceful congregates and tourists who come to celebrate Lennon's memory and the notable events of his time.

Summit Rock (83rd Street west of West Drive): This highest point in the park at 137 feet overlooks Central Park West. Relandscaped in 1996, the design features many native plantings and a circular summit that gives the sense of even greater altitudes. A serpentine rustic railing accents its entrance from the east.

Ross Pinetum (northwest corner of the Great Lawn): Planted in 1971 (a donation from Arthur Ross, a frequent park benefactor), the area features hundreds of pines representing a dozen species from around the world.

North Meadow Recreation Center (mid-park north of the 97th Street Transverse Road): A popular gathering center for handball and basketball players. Many community recreational programs unite the public with the park here. Courts are first-come, first-served except for scheduled events. Also the headquarters of Parks Enforcement Patrol (PEP) and Park Rangers' field headquarters.

Great Hill (between 107th and 108th Streets west of West Drive): This little-known open green space is a favorite of picnickers who have discovered it. It lies safely secluded within a border of woods with a ring of elms surrounding an open hilly lawn. Its circular gravel track was the carriage turnaround when the park terminated at this latitude and the hill featured a playground for children. During the Revolutionary War a British campsite occupied the hill; some artifacts are still buried beneath the lawn.

The Blockhouse (at the level of 108th Street and Adam Clayton Powell Jr. Boulevard/7th Avenue): The oldest structure in Central Park built in 1814 after the British invaded Stonington, Connecticut, on their way to Manhattan during the War of 1812. Volunteers from Columbia University and laborers from downtown scurried to erect the fortress out of local boulders and mount a cannon on top should the British assault the island. The Blockhouse awaits restoration at this writing and visitors should be accompanied by friends.

Appendix B

*Interesting Trees and Shrubs Not Mentioned
on the Walks*

TREES

(Numbers in parentheses refer to number of specimens found in *The
Central Park 1982 Tree Inventory.*)

Tree of heaven (*Ailanthus altissima*): considered a weed by
many, this tenacious tree displays attractive flowers, fruit, and
foliage year-round. (503)

Paper mulberry (*Broussonetia papyrifera*): a relative of the
red and white mulberries with velvety leaves and appealing
red-orange bark after a rain. (57)

Yellow-wood (*Cladrastis lutea*): medium size—to 50 feet—
with small white flowers borne in long clusters in late spring
followed by brown pea-pods in autumn. The common name
refers to the bright yellow heart-wood used as a dye in early
America. (16)

Japanese dogwood (*Cornus kousa*): small with showy, hor-
izontal sprays of white, four-petaled flowers in late June and
raspberry-shaped fruits in August. (7)

Kentucky coffee tree (*Gymnocladus dioicus*): large—to 90
feet—with ten-inch-long seed pods from September through
winter; the pods contain nuts once used as a bitter beverage by
American settlers and for roasting by Native Americans. (23)

Carolina silverbell (*Halsesia carolina*): handsome small
tree—to 20 feet—with white-striped silver bark and dainty
flowers shaped like snowdrops, in May. (19)

Black walnut (*Juglans nigra*): a favorite American tree noted for its lumber and tasty nuts encased in a thick green husk; recognized by the striking, dark, deeply furrowed bark. (23)

Black walnut

Golden rain (*Koelreuteria paniculata*): small Asian tree with numerous rich yellow blossoms that cover the ground like golden rain in early summer followed by yellow-green seed pods in late summer that resemble Chinese lanterns. (60)

American larch (*Larix laricina*): deciduous conifer with airy pyramidal form and dark, flaky bark. Important timber trees in the North, they look like dead pine trees in winter. (24)

American larch

Cucumber magnolia (*Magnolia acuminata*): northernmost and largest magnolia—70 feet high—with large blossoms often hidden by large leaves 10 inches long and 5 inches wide. Furrowed bark resembles bark of the ash tree. (70)

Sourwood (*Oxydendron arboreum*): exceptionally handsome small tree with 6–8-inch-long clusters of fragrant small flowers, similar to lilies-of-the-valley, which decorate the tree through midsummer and continue their landscape appeal as seed into early autumn. (12)

Empress (*Paulownia tomentosa*): fast-growing, short-lived dense tree with stunning 10-inch clusters of vanilla-scented blue flowers in spring. Easily confused with the catalpa in form and leaf, the Empress's woody fruit capsule and blue flowers distinguish it from the bean-shaped fruit and white flowers of the catalpa. (39)

Eastern cottonwood (*Populus deltoides*): a short-lived (80–100 years), fast-growing tall tree (70–90 feet high), with furrowed, dark, green-yellow bark and mature stature. Poplars in general have a dubious reputation for clogging drainpipes with their roots. The soft wood is a staple in the paper pulp industry. (28)

Eastern cottonwood

Japanese zelkova (*Zelkova serrata*): medium-to-large tree with vase-shaped form and leaves similar to American elm; used in some locations as a replacement for elms ravished by

Dutch elm disease. The light-gray bark often has whitish smudges. (13)

SHRUBS

Fountain buddleia (*Buddleia alternifolia*): especially prominent in the Conservatory Garden, this shrub offers conspicuous blue blossoms in late summer and is often referred to as the Butterfly Magnet.

Flowering quince (*Chaenomeles japonica*): a low shrub forming a thorny hedge in the Conservatory Garden. This native of the woods and mountains of Japan displays orange-scarlet flowers in late spring.

Forsythia (*Forsythia intermedia*): early April flowering hedge shrub with massive yellow blossoms that highlight the park's drives before its foliage appears and blends it into the background.

Oak-leaf hydrangea (*Hydrangea quercifolia*): this beautiful native hydrangea displays blossoms similar to many viburnums but possesses leaves distinctively shaped like the oaks. Displayed well along Rhododendron Mile and in the Conservatory Garden.

Common juniper (*Juniperis communis*): low evergreen with prickly, blue-green foliage, the oil of which has been used in perfumery and as incense in India. Used commonly as low accents in formal landscapes.

Common juniper

Inkberry (*Ilex glabra*): the variety "Compacta" is encountered on the 59th Street Pond Walk, but the nonhybridized inkberry—spindly, naturalized, and immature—can be seen best in winter along the southwest Loch past the second rustic bridge.

Leucothoe (*Leucothoe spp.*): low evergreen with foliage similar to rhododendron found around Cherry Hill. The small white flowers in May resemble those of the blueberries.

Spicebush (*Lindera benzoin*): native shrub with early yellow blossoms similar from a distance to forsythia. Crushed leaves and fruit emit strong, spicy fragrance. Most common in North Woods and the Ramble.

Privet (*Ligustrum spp.*): dense hedge shrub that becomes scraggly when not maintained, as is too often the case in Central Park. The tiny, fragrant white flowers in late June are appealing.

Japanese andromeda (*Pieris japonica*): a 3–5-foot shrub with delicate evergreen foliage and in mid-April showy clusters of small bell-shaped flowers that remain as decorative seeds well into summer. Found densely on the Conservatory Water Walk surrounding the Hans Christian Andersen statue.

Photinia (*Photinia villosa*): open shrub with leaves similar to Juneberry *Amelanchier, spp.,* but has larger, white blossoms, late April. A most effective shrub in groups, as at the south edge of the East Meadow along the 97th Street Transverse Road, where they add yellow and red luster to the autumnal foliage.

Fragrant sumac (*Rhus aromatica*): a low, straggly native shrub with trifoliate leaves similar to poison ivy to the untrained eye. Tiny yellow flowers appear before the leaves, which when crushed are aromatic. Interesting naturalizing plant found sparsely along the Bridle Trail around the reservoir and in North Woods.

Multiflora rose (*Rosa multiflora*): a dense and extremely invasive rosebush when outside the park, with appealing small white blossoms in June. Found in less formal locations inside the park.

Blueberry (*Vaccinium spp.*): mostly 1–3-foot spreading shrubs with small, bell-shaped white flowers in late April offering fruit in late summer that is quickly eaten by birds. Found sparsely in the park's woodlands.

Double-file viburnum (*Viburnum tomentosum*): one of the most stunning viburnums in flower, with rows of blossoms like creamy white bracelets drifting across its branches in early summer. In its native Japan and China it grows as scrub in the mountains. Found throughout the park.

Yellowroot (*Xanthorhiza simplicissima*): viney shrub to 3 feet tall with lacy foliage and delicate clusters of purplish flowers. Found in shady woods mostly around the north end of the park.

Appendix C

Common Birds Found in Central Park

Adapted from "The Birds of Central Park: An Annotated Checklist," a publication of the Central Park Conservancy; *The Falconer of Central Park,* by Donald Knowler; *Central Park Wildlife Inventory,* by John Hecklau; *Central Park: A History and Guide,* by Henry Hope Reed and Sophia Duckworth.

Year-round Residents

American Crow
Blue Jay
Mockingbird
Common Grackle
Northern Cardinal
Mourning Dove
Downy Woodpecker
Tufted Titmouse
Song Sparrow
House Finch
Mallard
Herring Gull
Ring-Billed Gull
Black-Crowned Night Heron
Robin
Domestic Pigeon (Rock Dove)

European Starling
House Sparrow

Annual Migrants

Warblers *(includes only the most common of nearly forty warbler species in Central Park)*
    Palm Warbler
    Yellow-rumped Warbler
    Northern Waterthrush
    Prairie Warbler
    Yellow Warbler
    Yellowthroat
    Black-throated Blue Warbler
    Ovenbird
    Canada Warbler
    Blackburnian Warbler
    Magnolia Warbler
Waterfowl *(common migrants and winter visitants)*
    Ruddy Duck
    Lesser Scaup
    Bufflehead
    Black Duck
    Canvasback
    Shoveler
    Gadwall
    Pied-billed Grebe
    Green-winged Teal
    Wood Duck
    Common Loon
Winter Visitants *(common interior birds)*
    White-throated Sparrow
    Dark-eyed Junco
    Swamp Sparrow

Rufous-sided Towhee
Brown-headed Cowbird
Pine Siskin
American Goldfinch
Purple Finch
Cedar Waxwing
White-breasted Nuthatch
Northern Flicker
Hairy Woodpecker

Appendix D

Bloom Times in Central Park

March

3RD WEEK: Red maple   *Acer rubrum*

4TH WEEK: American elm   *Ulmus americana*
              Winter honeysuckle   *Lonicera fragantissima*
              Daffodil   *Narcissus spp.*
              Korean rhododendron   *Rhododendron
                                                mucronnulatum*
              Lesser celandine   *Ranunculus ficaria*
              Pachysandra   *Pachysandra
                                                terminalis*
              Cornelian cherry   *Cornus mas*

April

1ST WEEK: Forsythia   *Forsythia X intermedia*
              Spicebush   *Lindera benzoin*
              Magnolia   *Magnolia spp.*

Lesser celandine	*Ranunculus ficaria*
Periwinkle	*Vinca minor*
Yellowroot	*Xanthorhiza simplicissima*
Trout lily	*Erythronium americana*

2ND WEEK:	Virginia bluebell	*Mertensia virginiana*
	Common blue violet	*Viola papilionacea*
	Norway maple	*Acer platanoides*
	Dandelion	*Taraxacum officinalis*

3RD WEEK:	Yoshino cherry	*Prunus yedoensis*
	Juneberry	*Amelanchier arborea*
	Quince	*Cydonia japonica*

4TH WEEK:	Crabapple	*Malus spp.*
	Tulip	*Tulipa spp.*
	Shadblow	*Amelanchier canadensis*
	Barberry	*Berberis spp.*
	Flowering dogwood	*Cornus florida*
	Redbud	*Cercis canadensis*
	Fothergilla	*Fothergilla gardeni*
	Blueberry	*Vaccinium corymbosum*
	Pin Cherry	*Prunus pensylvanica*

May

1ST WEEK:	Lilac	*Syringa spp.*
	Azalea	*Rhododendron spp.*
	Hawthorn	*Cratageus spp.*
	Jetbead	*Rhodotypos scandens*
	Geranium	*Geranium maculatum*

	Leatherleaf viburnum	*Viburnum rhytidophyllum*
	Koreanspice viburnum	*Viburnum carlesii*
2ND WEEK:	Doublefile viburnum	*Viburnum plicatum var. tomentosum*
	Blackhaw viburnum	*Viburnum prunifolium*
	Siebold viburnum	*Viburnum sieboldii*
	Horse chestnut	*Aesculus hippocastanum*
	Japanese wisteria	*Wisteria floribunda*
3RD WEEK:	European cranberry viburnum	*Viburnum opulus*
	American cranberry viburnum	*Viburnum trilobum*
	Columbine	*Aquilegia canadensis*
	Solomon's seal	*Polygonatum biflorum*
	Alumroot	*Heuchera americana*
	Black cherry	*Prunus serotina*
4TH WEEK:	Black locust	*Robinia pseudoacacia*
	Photinia	*Photinia serrulata*
	Catawba rhododendron	*Rhododendron catawbiense*
	Blueflag iris	*Iris versicolor*
	Mock orange	*Philadelphus spp.*
	Buttercup	*Ranunculus spp.*
	Arrowwood viburnum	*Viburnum dentatum*
	Mapleleaf viburnum	*Viburnum acerifolium*

June

1ST WEEK:	Arrowwood viburnum	*Viburnum dentatum*
	Mapleleaf viburnum	*Viburnum acerifolium*

	Cranberry viburnum	*Viburnum trilobum*
	Rose	*Rosa spp.*
	Mountain laurel	*Kalmia latifolia*
	Tree lilac	*Syringa reticulata*

2ND WEEK:	Elderberry	*Sambucus canadensis*
	Catalpa	*Catalpa speciosa*
	Coreopsis	*Coreopsis lancelota*
	Inkberry	*Ilex glabra*

3RD WEEK:	Oakleaf hydrangea	*Hydrangea quercifolia*
	Yarrow	*Daucus carota*
	Gray dogwood	*Cornus racemosa*
	Bayberry	*Myrica pensylvanica*

4TH WEEK:	Linden	*Tilia spp.*
	Milkweed	*Asclepias syriaca*
	Rosebay rhododendron	*Rhododendron maximum*
	Privet	*Lisustrum spp.*

July

| 1ST WEEK: | Bottlebrush buckeye | *Aesculus parviflora* |
| | Day lily | *Hemerocallis fulva* |

2ND WEEK:	Coneflower	*Echinacea spp.*
	Joe-pye weed	*Fupatorium purpureum*
	Bee balm	*Monarda fistulosa*
	Pickerel weed	*Pontederia cordata*
	Chicory	*Cichorium intybus*

| 3RD WEEK: | Cup-plant | *Silphium perfoliatum* |
| | Black-eyed Susan | *Rudbeckia hirta* |

	Virginia knotweed	*Polygonum virginia*
	Manhattan euonymous	*Euonymous "Manhattan"*
4TH WEEK:	Spreading euonymous	*Euonymous kiautschovicus*
	Cardinal flower	*Lobelia cardinalis*
	Horse nettle	*Solanum carolinense*
	Pepperbush	*Clethra ainifolia*

August

1ST WEEK:	Scholar tree	*Sophora japonica*
	Blue cardinal flower	*Lobelia siphilitica*
	Ragweed	*Ambrosia artemissifolia*
	Devil's walking stick	*Aralia spinosa*

September

1ST WEEK:	White wood aster	*Aster divaricatus*
	Goldenrod	*Solidago spp.*

Selected Bibliography

Barlow, Elizabeth, *The Central Park Book* (New York: The Central Park Task Force, 1981).

Coe, James, *Eastern Birds* (New York: Golden Press, 1994).

Collins, Henry Hill, Jr., *Complete Field Guide to American Wildlife* (New York: Harper & Brothers, 1959).

Cramer, Marianne, Judith Heintz, and Bruce Kelly, *Vegetation in Central Park* (Prepared for the Central Park Conservancy, 1984).

Graff, M. M., *The Ramble in Central Park* (Unpublished Report, 1979).

———, *Tree Trails in Central Park* (New York: Greensward Foundation, 1970).

Hecklau, John, *Central Park Wildlife Inventory* (Prepared for the Central Park Conservancy, 1981).

Kinkead, Eugene, *Central Park: The Birth, Decline and Renewal* (New York: W. W. Norton, 1990).

Kricher, John C., *Ecology of Eastern Forests* (New York: Houghton Mifflin, 1988).

Leopold, Aldo, *A Sand County Almanac* (New York: Oxford University Press, 1949).

Peterson, Roger Tory and Margaret McKenny, *A Field Guide to Wildflowers* (Boston: Houghton Mifflin, 1968).

Petrides, George A., *A Field Guide to Trees and Shrubs* (Boston: Houghton Mifflin, 1972).

Reed, Henry Hope and Sophia Duckworth, *Central Park: A History and Guide* (New York: Clarkson N. Potter, 1967).

Reed, Henry Hope, Robert M. McGee, and Esther Mippas, *Bridges of Central Park* (New York: Greensward Foundation, 1990).

Index

Entries in **boldface** refer to maps
and illustrations.